The
COMPLETE
GUIDE to
SELLING YOUR
BUSINESS

2ND EDITION

PAUL S SPERRY & BEATRICE H MITCHELL
EDITED BY ANDREW ROBERTS

Grant Thornton

RECOMMENDED BY

INSTITUTE OF DIRECTORS

**KOGAN
PAGE**

This book has been endorsed by the Institute of Directors.

The endorsement is given to selected Kogan Page books which the IoD recognises as being of specific interest to its members and providing them with up-to-date, informative and practical resources for creating business success. Kogan Page books endorsed by the IoD represent the most authoritative guidance available on a wide range of subjects including management, finance, marketing, training and HR.

Publisher's note

Every possible effort has been made to ensure that the information contained in this book is accurate at the time of going to press, and the publishers, authors and editor cannot accept responsibility for any errors or omissions, however caused. No responsibility for loss or damage occasioned to any person acting, or refraining from action, as a result of the material in this publication can be accepted by the editor, the publisher or any of the authors.

This book provides an overview of the subject of selling a business. It is presented on the understanding that it provides general background information only. If legal, tax or accounting, or other expert assistance is required, the services of a competent professional should be sought.

For the sake of simplicity, the authors have used 'he' to stand for 'he or she' throughout this book.

First published in the United States by Upstart Publishing Company, Inc, Dover, NH 03820 in 1992
First published in Great Britain by Kogan Page in 1999
Second edition 2004
Paperback edition 2005

Kogan Page Limited
120 Pentonville Road
London N1 9JN
United Kingdom
www.kogan-page.co.uk

The views expressed in this book are those of the authors, and are not necessarily the same as those of the Institute of Directors.

British Library Cataloguing in Publication Data

A CIP record for this book is available from the British Library.

ISBN 0 7494 4457 6

For Sarah, William and Frances:
our beloved children

Contents

Introduction   1

1.   Why sell?   5
2.   A sale versus a flotation   23
3.   What your company is worth: a question of value   31
4.   Issues to address before considering a sale   43
5.   How advisers fit into the picture   55
6.   The sale process   69
7.   Negotiating and structuring the optimal deal   85
8.   The sale and purchase agreement and completion of the
      deal   107
9.   Case study: Advanced Technologies Ltd   121

Appendices
I   Sample confidentiality agreements   139
II   Sample heads of agreement   147
III   Sample due diligence checklist   153
IV   Table of contents of a share sale and purchase
      agreement   159
V   Table of contents of an asset purchase agreement   165

Glossary   169

Index   177

Other titles available from Kogan Page in the Business Enterprise Guide series:

Published in association with *The Sunday Times* and the Institute of Directors

The Business Enterprise Handbook: A complete guide to achieving profitable growth for all entrepreneurs and SMEs, Colin Barrow, Robert Brown and Liz Clarke

The Business Plan Workbook, **Fourth Edition**, Colin Barrow, Paul Barrow and Robert Brown

The Company Secretary's Handbook: A guide to the duties and responsibilities, Third Edition, Helen Ashton

The Customer Service Workbook, Neville Lake and Kristin Hickey

Do Your Own Market Research, Third Edition, Paul Hague

E-Business for the Small Business: Making a profit from the Internet, John G Fisher

Financial Management for the Small Business, Fifth Edition, Colin Barrow

Forming a Limited Company, Eighth Edition, Patricia Clayton

How to Prepare a Business Plan, Fourth Edition, Edward Balckwell

Law for the Small Business, Tenth Edition, Patricia Clayton

Managing People in a Small Business, John Stredwick

Practical Marketing and PR for the Small Business, Second Edition, Moi Ali

Running a Home-based Business, Second Edition, Diane Baker

Starting a Successful Business, Fourth Edition, Michael J Morris

The Strategic Planning Workbook, Neville Lake

Successful Marketing for the Small Business: A practical guide, Fifth Edition, Dave Patten

The above titles are available from all good bookshops. To obtain further information, please contact the publisher at the address below:

Kogan Page Limited
120 Pentonville Road
London N1 9JN
United Kingdom
Tel: +44 (0) 20 7278 0433
Fax: +44 (0) 20 7837 6348
www.kogan-page.co.uk

About the authors

Paul Sperry and Beatrice Mitchell are principals in the New York-based investment banking firm of Sperry, Mitchell & Company, which specialises in representing small to medium-sized private companies seeking a sale or merger. The two have over 50 years of collective experience in the merger and acquisition field, mostly concentrating on transactions involving middle-market companies.

Paul S Sperry received his BA from Trinity College and an MA from Columbia University. Prior to establishing Sperry, Mitchell & Co, he was President of another small investment bank in New York. He is on the board of a number of private companies and non-profit organisations.

Beatrice H Mitchell received her BA from Yale University and an MBA from Columbia. She has had significant prior experience in both the banking and advertising fields. Ms Mitchell is on the board of numerous non-profit and community organisations.

Both are recognised experts in the field of mergers and acquisitions, and are frequent participants and featured speakers at M&A seminars, trade associations and industry conferences. Ms Mitchell is a regular lecturer at Columbia University Business School.

Both Mr Sperry and Ms Mitchell have been widely quoted by the press, most recently in *The Wall Street Journal*, *Forbes*, *Business Week* and *USA Today*, and on CNN National Public Radio. They are also frequent contributors to business and academic publications.

About the editor

Andrew Roberts is a partner in Grant Thornton Corporate Finance, based in Birmingham, England. He has been advising the owners of medium-sized companies and businesses since 1983.

He qualified as a Chartered Accountant in 1977 and became a partner in 1983. He is a regular speaker for the Institute of Directors. He devised and created the Web site companiesforsale.uk.com and specialises in advising companies with a value of £3 million plus.

'There is no man who is not in some degree a merchant; who has not something to buy or something to sell.'

Samuel Johnson

Introduction

Recently, we were involved in the sale of a medium-sized distributor of pneumatic tools. The company had been run very successfully for over 20 years by its two owners. While both enjoyed working and were in good health, they had reached the point in life where they wanted to work less hard, take more time off and enjoy the fruits of their labour.

Though both men had families, none of their children worked in the company, nor did any of them have any interest in joining. The company had a capable second tier of management, but there was no one who could really run the business besides the two owners. After much thought, both men decided that the only sensible alternative open to them was to sell.

Having arrived at the decision to sell, the owners next had the difficult task of figuring out how to go about it. They did not want to talk to their competitors, for obvious concerns of confidentiality. They had some vague ideas as to other companies that might have an interest, but they had no idea how to approach them.

By chance, we met both owners at a social function, and they told us of their dilemma. A number of conversations and meetings ensued, and we were retained to handle the sale of their business. The search and negotiation process took six months, during which time both owners were exposed to numerous potential acquirers offering various types of transactions. The company was eventually sold to two wealthy private investors, one of whom wanted to run the business. After a two-month transitional period, both clients retired completely from the business, satisfying one of their original goals.

Over lunch a few weeks after the transaction was completed, one of the owners remarked to us that he had no idea what he was getting into when he first addressed the idea of selling. Though he had been a capable businessman who had built a successful company, he felt totally unprepared as to what to expect in selling his company. He did not know what a Heads of Agreement was, or what to look for in a Sale and Purchase Agreement. He did not even know where to get good, competent advice on these matters. Our client went on to suggest that it would have been quite helpful if he had a guide at the beginning of the process that would have educated and prepared him for what was to follow.

That conversation was the genesis of this book. As advisers dealing with private company owners on a daily basis, we have come to realise that very few business owners have a proper understanding of matters relating to selling or acquiring a company.

This book is addressed to owners of private small to medium-sized companies, who compose the backbone of the domestic economy. We wrote this book to provide you with good nuts and bolts advice on how to go about selling your business. The book addresses all of the fundamental questions and challenges involved in putting together a deal for your company. We also recommend this book to accountants, lawyers, business consultants and even potential buyers, so that they too can have a better understanding of how the process works and how deals get done.

Selling is one of the most important decisions you will ever make regarding your company. It is also one of the most important personal economic decisions you will face. And yet, all too often, owners of private companies will enter into negotiations without any proper planning, totally unprepared for the many complex issues involved in selling.

As is true with most things in life, planning pays. Selling a business should warrant at least as much planning and preparation as any other major corporate undertaking, such as a factory extension or a new product introduction. You need to give this project the time, effort and attention that it deserves.

All too often, private business owners view selling in a negative light; they consider selling only when in dire trouble. In this book, we attempt to dispel this specious notion. As you accumulate profits in your business, it is essential that you periodically evaluate the option of selling to reclaim those assets. In addition, selling can help you to better position your company for growth by feeding off of the capital and capabilities of a larger parent. Rather than a negative move, selling can truly be a liberating step for both you and your company.

The main point that we stress throughout this book is that selling requires selling. In the end, selling your company is no different than selling any other product: you need to plan your strategy, position your product, and then aggressively take action. If you take a cavalier attitude and ignore your customer (in this case, the buyer), then you will most probably fail – like all other companies that refuse to respond to their customers.

This book should serve as a guide to steer you through each phase of the selling process, providing the techniques necessary to negotiate a good deal, while highlighting the common mistakes and problems to avoid. The format of this book follows the basic sequence of the selling process, from planning a strategy and establishing a value, to structuring a deal and negotiating the agreements.

Mergers, disposals and acquisitions are, by their very nature, very technical creatures, involving many complex legal, accounting and tax issues. We have attempted to make this book as user-friendly and accessible as possible, though at times we need to digress into technical areas. You need not retain all of the financial or legal meanderings to get a grasp of the process and what it entails.

Given the complexity of the various matters related to acquisitions and disposals, it is important to realise that this book cannot possibly take the place of your accountant or legal adviser in providing expert advice on your specific situation. This book is meant only to introduce general concepts and provide an overview of the process. Selling your business is too important a matter not to get the best advice you can.

There are no domestic markets today; all markets have become international. This is especially true of mergers and acquisitions, where it has become just as likely that the ultimate buyer of your company will come from across a national border as across town. The contents of this book are global in nature and relate as much to markets in Europe as in America. The base of sellers and the universe of buyers has become as international as the markets. While there are a few different 'wrinkles' depending on culture or legal systems, the basic message of this book is as relevant to a business owner in Los Angeles as in Liverpool.

We provide many examples in this book, some based on actual clients, some based on composites. We appreciate those former clients who allowed us to profile their situations in order to emphasise salient points.

Certain people have been very generous with their time and efforts in helping us put this book together. Special thanks should go to Cynthia Lam who toiled long and hard in helping us to research and write the manuscript. Andrew Roberts of Grant Thornton reviewed and edited this edition especially for the United Kingdom. We also tip our hat to David Mitchell for introducing us to Spencer Smith at Kogan Page, who has been very understanding and accommodating throughout this process.

Lastly, we owe gratitude to the hundreds of business owners we have talked to or worked with over the years. It is through our experience with these owners that we were able to write this book. In essence, they are really the authors.

1 *Why sell?*

Private business owners decide to sell their companies for a variety of reasons. Though each owner probably considers his circumstances to be unique, most actually share similar concerns and motivations. In this chapter, we highlight many of the common reasons why owners consider selling. We also explain how you can determine the ideal time to sell in order to achieve the most advantageous deal.

Reasons for selling

If you are like most business owners, you will probably consider selling your company for one of, or a combination of, the following five reasons:

1. *Retirement:* you want to retire or to reduce the amount of time you spend working in your business.
2. *Succession:* there exists no family member or logical second-tier manager to take over your company.
3. *Diversity of assets:* as most of your net worth is tied up in your company, you want to diversify your assets, as well as gain some liquidity.
4. *Capital for growth:* you see a need for additional external capital to continue to grow your company.
5. *Association with a larger firm:* you seek the broader distribution channels, marketing strengths or manufacturing efficiencies that a larger firm can offer.

1. Retirement or a reduction of time spent in the business

You probably believe that you work far harder than your friends or acquaintances who do not own their own company. In most cases, you are right. Indeed, it is precisely your commitment and devotion to your business that enabled it to flourish in the first place. Many owners believe that if they are not the first one to arrive in the morning and the last to leave at night, their business will suffer. While maintaining a frantic pace of life may be challenging, stimulating and fun (and, indeed, necessary in building a business), at some point most owners decide that they want to slow down.

A few years ago, we represented Robert Spencer, the owner of Spensports, a large chain of discount sporting goods stores located in the Midlands. After a life-long career working for major retailers, Bob Spencer decided to establish his own business in his early 60s. In just five years, he built a business generating over £50 million of revenues from ten retail locations. While he had assembled an excellent management team, Bob Spencer remained the driving force behind the company.

A tall and commanding man, Bob was well regarded in the sporting goods community as a keen competitor and an excellent merchant. He still travelled regularly to Hong Kong to oversee the buying for the company.

When we first met him, Bob told us that he would never have considered selling if he were ten years younger. He saw unlimited opportunities for his new retailing concept and believed that Spensports was on the verge of exploding growth. However, having toiled through the start-up phase of the company, Bob just did not have the spark to continue at the same pace to grow it. He eventually decided that his only alternative was to sell the business.

After considering numerous offers for his company, Bob Spencer decided to sell Spensports to a large Stock Exchange-listed retailer. While there were several reasons he preferred his eventual buyer over others, the major consideration was the fact that the acquirer had a strong and deep management team in the speciality retailing area. Immediately after the sale was completed, the buyer transferred one of their senior retailing executives to Spensports to assume the management of the company. Bob Spencer did not immediately retire, but the sale did enable him to scale back his

Is your business at a crossroads? Not sure which way to turn for the financial advice that will shape your future?
Then **Grant Thornton Corporate Finance**...

Grant Thornton ⬥

...will lead you along the best route. Let us help you put together the bespoke financial package that will help your business grow in the right direction.

For more information contact:
Andrew Roberts
Grant Thornton
Enterprise House
115 Edmund Street
Birmingham B3 2HJ
T 0121 232 5210
E andrew.roberts@gtuk.com
W www.grant-thornton.co.uk
W www.companiesforsale.uk.com

Advisers to the independently minded

UK member of Grant Thornton International
© 2004 Grant Thornton. All rights reserved.

"The **disposal** of a business can be a complicated affair, especially when you've had no previous experience of the process. And having someone to explain everything in…

…layman's terms so that we understood exactly what was going on, left us feeling in control of the situation and confident of a successful outcome,"

Peter Carolan,
Managing Director of
Kennedy Construction.

Peter continues: "I first came into contact with Grant Thornton Corporate Finance in 1997 when I led an MBO of a family business founded in 1962. Since then whenever we have sought the advice of the corporate finance team they have been fantastic and with their help we have more than doubled in size in three years.

"But having reached a crossroad in our business development, we had to decide whether to get a much larger financial backer, or go for a trade sale. We decided to run both options at the same time and ended up opting for a trade sale."

For more information contact:
Andrew Roberts
Grant Thornton
Enterprise House
115 Edmund Street
Birmingham B3 2HJ
T 0121 232 5210
E andrew.roberts@gtuk.com
W www.grant-thornton.co.uk
W www.companiesforsale.uk.com

Grant Thornton 🐴

Grant Thornton Corporate Finance helped to:

- research the market
- line up potential buyers
- advise on what to include in the sales information memorandum
- lead and negotiate the deal.

"When the deal became complicated, the corporate finance team came up with a **flexible solution** that suited both vendor and purchaser."

Peter explains: "Whilst the majority of the shares in Kennedy were owned by the management team, the original Kennedy family held preference shares and as a result we were unable to produce some of the warranties that the vendor required.

"This could have been a potential deal breaker but Grant Thornton Corporate Finance managed the situation and came up with a viable solution that suited all concerned.

"By keeping us on track the corporate finance team ensured that our business plan was – and remained – extremely attractive. As a consequence we were very satisfied with the outcome, which resulted in a sale to Alfred McAlpine plc for £52.2million."

You need to walk on tip-toe when passing a business on to the next generation. The Grant Thornton PRIMA service...

"Our father was well past normal retirement age but found it difficult to give up and be certain of the future both for himself and the business."

Eimear Begley
O'Sullivan Shoes Limited

The overlap between the family and the business needs active management and our PRIMA service has been designed to help you take steps to tackle the issues that are important to you and your business.

Grant Thornton, recognising the needs of family businesses, developed the PRIMA service which is delivered worldwide by our consultants.

PRIMA, People and Relationship Issues in ManAgement, first identifies the issues and potential conflicts and then finds solutions, which are tailored to your overall needs and circumstances. In our experience the issues confronted by a family

with regard to the ownership of the business fall into the following factors:

- succession planning
- remuneration planning
- equity ownership by family members
- family members not involved in the business
- introducing and rewarding non-family executives
- retirement and estate planning
- bringing family members into the business
- strategic planning
- financial structure
- preserving wealth
- resolving conflicts
- the family creed.

For more information on the PRIMA service contact:
Paul Andrews
Grant Thornton
Grant Thornton House
Melton Street
Euston Square
London NW1 2EP
T 0870 991 2720
E paul.andrews@gtuk.com
W www.grant-thornton.co.uk

...helped Eimear and her sisters make the right steps to take control of the business started by their father.

Grant Thornton

Recognising that the culture, structure and characteristics of each family are different, our PRIMA consultants can help you to understand the issues in the context of your business. Our specialist consultants are adept at dealing with family business, wherever they are in the world – we operate in over 600 offices in more than 100 countries.

Whilst the family and business relationship may be unique, it is likely that the issues you are facing have similarities with those experienced by numerous other family businesses. We have been able to help many of them through these sensitive situations.

To find out more about how Grant Thornton could bring its unique approach to your business, contact Paul Andrews to arrange an appointment with a PRIMA consultant near you.

Eimear Begley, Caroline MacCurtain and Derville O'Sullivan are directors and owners of O'Sullivan Shoes Limited. The company was founded by their father Ned O'Sullivan in 1939 in Limerick, Ireland. It retails shoes for children and adults through its shops in the city.

time and involvement in the day-to-day operations. The result was that Bob could remain active in the business, without the on-going responsibilities or headaches of running the business.

Once a sole owner of a company decides to retire or reduce his time in a business, a sale of the company is the natural path to take. However, a sale is also a logical alternative when only one of many partners decides to retire and the others cannot or do not want to assume the burden of buying out the retiring partner. Quite often, partners who want to continue with the business cannot possibly afford to buy out a departing partner at fair market value. Even if those remaining could afford the buyout, they are often reluctant to shoulder the entire responsibility of running the company, especially if they are incurring significant debt to buy out the departing partner. In such instances, a sale of the company can not only provide liquidity to all partners but can also be structured in a way that provides on-going jobs, equity participation and incentives to the remaining partners.

2. Succession concerns

One of the most common problems all owners face is the question of who will succeed them when they retire or are forced to leave because of illness. Most owners are undoubtedly the inspiration and main driving force behind their company. As such, they find it difficult to delegate responsibility to others. Even when owners can delegate responsibility, most small businesses simply do not need layers of senior management, nor can they support the overhead. Undoubtedly, you are tremendously important to the success of your business. Should anything serious happen to you, your company would suffer dramatically from lack of direction and stability.

Recently, we were exposed to an extreme example of a succession problem. We had been in touch with an owner of a manufacturing concern for many years. While he appeared interested in selling, he never had the time to focus his attention on the matter. This owner was in his early 60s and apparently in good health; the issue of selling never seemed especially pressing to him.

After many months of no contact, the owner's son eventually called us. Unfortunately, his father had suddenly dropped dead of a heart attack, leaving the company with no senior management in place. The son had been forced to quit his job, uproot his family to move back to his home town, and take over the running of the company, for which he was ill-prepared. The son had grown up in the business, but he had never actually assumed any management role. Naturally, he was anxious to sell the company as quickly as possible, at a significantly reduced value. Needless to say, a more far-sighted succession plan would have prevented such a difficult situation. By not planning better, the owner both unsettled his son's life and greatly diminished the value of the business (and thus the estate for his wife).

Many small business owners equate success with the creation of a family dynasty. They founded their company to be 'the family business', to be passed down from one generation to the next, providing both a familial bond and economic prosperity. Yet, reality displays quite a different picture. Studies by both Cranfield School of Management and Grant Thornton, within their PRIMA service – People and Relationship Issues in Management – show that only about 25 per cent of private businesses are passed from one generation to the next, and less than one in ten makes it to a third generation. Regardless of a founder's grand plans, he must eventually face the fact that, more often than not, his business will not be passed on to the next generation.

Most children have neither an interest in, nor a proclivity for, the family business. Just as likely, an owner's children are not the most capable candidates to take over the reins of his company. If an owner has two children who work for the family business and one child is clearly the more competent, promoting one over the other may cause severe problems. Similarly, there may be a competent non-family member who should rightfully succeed the owner as Managing Director, even though a son may argue that it is his birthright to succeed to the MD's job. In all of these cases, selling may provide a rational and fair solution for succession issues.

We recently acted on behalf of a company that was owned by two brothers, aged 38 and 43, and their 55-year old uncle. The two brothers were effectively running the company; their uncle had significantly reduced both his responsibilities and the time he spent in the business. The uncle owned one-half of the company's shares; the two brothers each owned 25 per cent. The uncle was interested in selling his shares and, within a short period of time, retiring.

The easy and logical solution would have been for the two nephews to buy out their uncle's share. The company had an available bank facility that could have been used to finance such an acquisition. On-going management was not an issue, as the two brothers could clearly run the company without their uncle. When we put this proposal to the family, there was an uncomfortable pause in the conversation. Later, the uncle took us aside and explained the situation. The younger brother was, in fact, much the stronger of the two. While the two brothers got along quite well, the older brother refused to participate in an acquisition if he could not be in charge. The older brother just could not bring himself to take a junior position to his younger brother. Hence, the three decided to sell the entire company to an outside party.

Establishing a protégé or a strong second tier of management obviously helps to address succession problems. However, in reality, this 'sharing of power' is often difficult to effect. Recently, we worked with a leading manufacturer of consumer items. The company was owned by two very able brothers, whose father had started the firm 50 years earlier. After 40 years in the business themselves, the brothers decided they wanted to scale back their direct involvement. A decision was made to search for a management team of experienced industry people to run their company. After a thorough search, they hired several executives, all of whom had an impressive background working for larger companies, and granted them share options to incentivise them.

The brothers immediately began to work part-time, allowing the new team to take over the reins of the business. They initially vowed to yield full financial and operating responsibility to the new managers; yet, over time, the brothers began to question or review every decision. All significant policy changes were resisted.

Six months after bringing in the new team, the brothers found themselves worrying about the business as much, if not more, than when they actually ran the company. After all, they still owned the company's equity and still remained the ones most directly affected by bad business decisions. Thus, it almost came as a relief when management's decision to diversify into a new market failed. After a year of deteriorating profits, the brothers fired or demoted all of their new managers and resumed running the company.

After their failed experience with 'professional' managers, the brothers decided that the only acceptable path to retirement would be a complete sale to outsiders. By selling, the brothers would be transferring the search for the 'right' management team and the equity risk of that decision to the buyer.

Owners are often faced with situations where they have built their company to a certain level of sales and market share, only to feel that they require managers with greater experience or different talents to take their company to the next plateau.

Two owners of a UK-based medical products company recently provided a specific example of this. The two founders started their company after long careers with a large medical products company. The one owner's forte was marketing; the other provided the engineering talent. In five years, their company grew to over £20 million in annual revenues. Both were proud of their accomplishments and clearly capable of guiding a profitable, growing company. However, both also felt unsettled with their new roles as executive officers of a quickly growing company. Each felt more comfortable and capable in their respective areas of marketing and engineering. So, they sought to sell their company to a party that would assume the strategic planning and operating responsibilities, while allowing both men the chance to concentrate instead on their strengths.

3. Diversification of assets

Perhaps the most common reason for owners to consider selling their company is the desire to increase their liquidity and diversify their assets. Private companies are generally very illiquid investments; no ready markets provide for a quick sale of part or all of a private company. Generally, profits must be ploughed back into a company to cover increased debtors or stock levels, or to purchase additional equipment. Thus, most of a private company's 'return' is actually reinvested back into an already illiquid investment.

Similarly, with most of your net worth retained in your business, you constantly risk your financial position with each major business decision or market development. A major plant expansion or new product development always brings with it new or greater risk. With all of your proverbial eggs in one basket, you may eventually tire of constantly risking your financial security on your company's continued prosperity.

Most private companies are founded on relatively small amounts of capital. Thus, early on, a business owner risks very little except his time and effort in building his business. In the early years of any business's evolution, growth almost demands risk. Because start-ups are worth relatively little, owners are generally quite willing to place their business on the line to achieve growth. Yet, as businesses mature, generate a significant capital base and evolve into major assets, many owners become more and more reticent to continually risk their company with each major new strategic move.

Selling your business allows you to bring some liquidity and diversification to your holdings, and to more rationally disperse your net worth among many asset classes. You can lessen your dependence on the continued success of your company and, at the same time, be in a position to enjoy your wealth.

We recently worked with the owners of a precision aluminium casting operation. The company was extremely profitable; however, the three owners felt obliged to continually reinvest all of their profits in new plant and equipment to remain competitive. While the three received salaries commensurate with their jobs, they did not have much disposable wealth. Their personal net worths were impressive, on paper. None felt particularly wealthy, however, as all of their net worth was tied up in the company. Should their business fortunes reverse, they feared, most of their wealth would disappear.

A sale allowed the owners to make their holdings 'liquid' and to realise a return on their years of effort. All three owners stayed on in their same capacities and continued to run the company as before. However, their personal bank accounts were such that should anything ever happen to the company, they could retire quite comfortably and never work again.

This example is far from an anomaly; in our experience, most owners *do* stay on to run their company after they have been sold, with many buyers requiring a handover period of at least 12 months. Subsequently many of the ex-owners believe that they are actually better managers after a sale than when they owned their company. No longer do they feel that they are putting their company (and thus their net worth) on the line each time they make a new strategic decision. Consequently, they feel free to take the prudent and appropriate risks that they might not have otherwise made had they continued to own their company.

4. Expansion capital

Companies may require additional capital. If they are growing quickly, owners may find that their cash demands outpace their resources. It is not uncommon for a quickly growing company to suddenly fail due to its own weight because it could not meet its growing cash needs. By definition, growth means increased stock and debtors. In addition, an expanding business requires continued investment in plant, equipment, training, advertising, distribution and an administrative and sales staff. Many small companies do not generate enough earnings internally to keep up with growing capital demands. Banks, the traditional source of funding for small companies, are generally reluctant to lend enough capital to maintain aggressive growth rates. Banks are constrained by formal ratios and lending covenants, which necessarily focus more on downside conservatism than growth possibilities.

Our prior examination of the Spensports chain provides an interesting example of a growing company's capital needs outstripping its internal capabilities. When the company was sold, it operated ten stores, all in the Midlands. Through internally generated cash and bank borrowings, the company had the financial resources available to open approximately three stores a year. However, in the fiercely competitive business of speciality retailing, Spensports' management knew that they needed to move quickly to establish themselves. Theirs was a unique marketing concept, but one that could be easily replicated by another company if they did not take the initiative to grow rapidly and establish a 'critical mass'.

The owner, Bob Spencer, quickly determined that only with an injection of outside money could he properly capitalise on the market opportunities. His sale of the company helped him to realise his goal; in the three years subsequent to the sale, Spensports grew from 10 stores to over 40, with a large share of each regional market in which they operated. It would have taken over a decade for the company to have achieved that growth through internally generated cash, if they could have achieved it at all.

5. Association with a larger company

Acquirers can bring more to private companies than just capital. Larger, more diverse companies can bring intangible advantages such as: wider and more developed sales and distribution channels; a larger, more sophisticated advertising and marketing capability; manufacturing and administrative efficiencies; and engineering and technical support. While these intangible advantages are rarely the main motivation for an owner to sell, they often become quite important once they are discovered.

One of our clients, a manufacturer of processing equipment for the petroleum industry, found that revenues could double in one year by switching from the company's manufacturer's representatives to the acquirer's direct marketing channels. Likewise, a recent client in the tyre distribution business found that administrative costs such as accounting, insurance and office staff costs dropped by 50 per cent after the firm was acquired.

Timing

One last factor you should consider prior to deciding to sell is the timing of a sale. Timing is a subject not often addressed or discussed by owners, but it is perhaps one of the most important factors in terms of successfully selling a business.

Like the stock and property markets, the markets for private companies rise and fall. It is important to be cognisant of the relative strengths of the markets in setting goals for a sale of a business. Clearly, by timing a sale to coincide with a strong market, you improve your chances of achieving your price and other objectives. There are three major elements to consider in the timing of a sale: 1) the macro or general economic environment; 2) the outlook of your company's industry; and 3) the relative prospects and performance of your company in particular.

Like biorhythms, the ideal time to consider a sale is when the prospects of all three are rising and the outlook remains healthy. Yet, as in biorhythms, it is rather rare that one can find a perfect time when all three indicators are just about to reach their apex. Thus, timing becomes more of an art than a science, anticipating which of the three factors will matter most to potential acquirers in the marketplace.

Buyers' psychology, not unlike consumers' psychology, is subject to general perceptions of the state of the world. Just as the stock market will often rise or fall depending on world affairs, interest from potential acquirers is often dependent on external matters and events.

Turning first to the general economic matters, it is obvious that one of the best times to consider selling is when the economy is experiencing sustained growth, low unemployment, a good trade balance and a rising stock market. Indeed, over the past five decades, there has been a high correlation between general economic growth and merger and acquisition activity. Times of generally stable growth and low interest rates correspond favourably to healthy acquisition markets and, thus, healthy pricing. Times of a stagnant economy or rising interest rates have lowered demand for acquisitions and resulted in lower overall values.

During most of the 1970s, the world economies were generally stagnant, interest rates were running at double-digit rates, unemployment was high, and most of the international stock markets were depressed. Large corporations were, in general, unenthusiastic about buying companies – most were more concerned about stabilizing their own businesses than growing or diversifying through acquisitions. Thus, the 1970s were a period of weak demand for companies, resulting in a stagnant acquisition market and depressed values. Many very healthy and successful firms generated tepid interest and weak pricing. Those that could often chose to delay selling their business.

The 1980s presented a much different picture: interest rates were as low as half what they had been in the 1970s, stock markets rebounded dramatically, and the world's GNP again grew at a strong rate. All of these positive economic indicators generated optimistic perceptions as to the market. Optimism increased demand: merger activity involving private companies doubled from 1979 to 1989. Correspondingly, the average price/earnings ratio paid for acquisition targets doubled in the same period. Many companies that would have attracted only low levels of interest in the 1970s were suddenly in the enviable position of having several good offers from which to choose.

The 1990s was a decade of contrasts. The early part of the decade suffered from a worldwide recession and a hangover caused by over-leverage in the financial markets. The result was a soft merger and acquisition market, and a corresponding dip in relative prices. By mid-decade, however, as the world's economies started to grow once again, and corporations began to focus on the internationalisation of markets, merger and acquisition activity began to blossom. Rising share prices and a huge availability of equity and debt money drove activity and pricing to record levels.

The change of millennium has seen a significant change in the economic outlook. The stock market FTSE100 peaked at 6930 in December 1999 and dropped steadily over the next three years to 3940 in December 2002. A number of external factors have reduced business confidence and created uncertainty. The tragic events of 11 September 2001, the Iraq War and the spread of the SARS epidemic all affected international trade and forward planning. The collapse of major companies such as Enron and Marconi added to the general antipathy. Many companies that had expansion plans decided to 'put them on ice' and sought instead to maintain liquidity.

The impact of the above reduced the number of deals that happened, and reduced the prices that were achieved. For those deals that did happen, they took much longer to complete, as purchasers were much more stringent in their due diligence.

The same general market perceptions that apply to macro factors also apply to the overall health of a company's industry. When an industry is growing and shows signs of continued prosperity, it reflects well on all companies in that industry. Unfortunately, the converse is also true. A receding tide lowers all boats, and a splendid company within a sick industry will be running against the tide in convincing potential acquirers of its desirability. Of course, if an industry is notoriously cyclical, such as housing or capital equipment, an owner should consider selling while the industry is expanding. Once the contraction begins, he may have to wait through another turn of the cycle to generate significant interest in his business.

Returning to the Spensports example for a moment, Bob Spencer took advantage of growing interest in the speciality retailing field to determine the appropriate time to market his company. Many large public retailers were trading at high multiples and viewed speciality retailing as a high-growth area for diversification. By timing his sale to coincide with strong market interest, Bob Spencer was able to maximise the eventual price for his business.

Another example was the owner of a company that produced drill bits for the oil industry. In the early 1980s, after a considerable run-up in oil prices, he decided to sell his company. All the major oil companies were very keen on locking up a source of supply for bits, because replacement parts had become hard to source. After playing many competing suitors against one another, the company was sold for a very high price to an industry buyer.

One year after the sale, the seller's friend decided that he, too, wanted to sell his company, which provided services to the off-shore oil industry. The catalyst for the sale was the great deal he saw our client get for his company. However, just as the owner of the service company decided to sell, the bottom fell out of the oil market. Drilling for oil dried up. Though the company had a number of attractive contracts and continued to prosper in the early years of the oil downturn, the market ignored his company completely, primarily because it was in what was perceived as an unattractive industry. After a year of marketing the company, we could find no buyers, even at a very low price. We finally advised our client to wait until the oil business rebounded before once again considering a sale.

The last and most vital factor to consider in weighing the timing of a sale is the specific performance and prospects of the company being sold. The ideal time to consider selling is when current performance is good, and prospects appear even better. Just as banks are most eager to lend money when a company has no immediate need for it, acquirers tend to be most interested in companies that are not under the gun to sell and that have no clouds on the horizon. It is safe to assume that most buyers are at least as prescient and intuitive as sellers. Buyers can generally ascertain when a business's fortunes are about to turn downwards.

When you sell a company that still appears to have plenty of opportunity and momentum, you can sell positive future prospects and therefore command a generous price. If questions exist as to future growth or profitability, or a downturn or loss is inevitable, acquirers will tend to focus on the short-term problems at the exclusion of the past performance or other inherent merits of the business.

A steady track record of profitability and growth will help to convince an acquirer that the trend will continue. From a value point of view, it is often quite advantageous for you to take the time to address and fix problems rather than accept the inevitable discounts you will face in selling a business with an uncertain future. Indeed, it is a fact of the marketplace that acquirers often overpay for well-run businesses promising good growth and severely discount poorly performing companies.

One of the most serious errors you can make is trying to squeeze the last pound out of your growth trend, leaving nothing to the potential acquirers. To pay a high price, acquirers have to believe that they are buying into a flourishing business. Markets and business conditions change too dramatically for you ever to be able to time a sale at the exact 'top' of the curve.

For most companies, the opportunity to clinch a great deal is a fleeting one; you must be prepared to act when all the signals are right. For that reason, even if a sale of the business is not an immediate goal, you should still periodically examine your business and its prospects in the market. This exercise will show you how the market might view and value your business. It will also allow you to better understand the dynamics of how changes in the market or in your business performance will influence the relative attractiveness of your company and its value.

2 *A sale versus a flotation*

You will eventually reach a point where you must make a vital decision regarding the future of your business. Should you hold onto your highly illiquid and risky investment and expand your company alone, reaping all the benefits for yourself? Or, alternatively, should you take steps to increase your liquidity and lessen your risks, giving up some future profits in the process?

This dilemma often propels a private company owner down one of two paths: a flotation on a stock market (also known as an initial public offering (IPO)) or a sale. In this chapter, we will examine these two options and discuss the differing solutions they provide regarding risk, liquidity and growth.

In the United Kingdom there are two main stock markets. There are significant differences between them, which are too detailed for the purpose of this book; however this is a thumbnail outline.

The Official List of the London Stock Exchange is the stock market usually referred to by commentators. It is fully regulated by the UK Listing Authority, and the prices and volumes of shares traded are shown on a daily (indeed almost real time) basis. This Main Market is usually appropriate for larger companies: say, those with a total market capitalisation value of more than £100 million.

The Alternative Investment Market of the London Stock Exchange, known as AIM, is usually appropriate for smaller companies with a value from £2 million upwards. This market is under the jurisdiction of the Stock Exchange. The rules for entry are more appropriate for smaller, growth-oriented companies. Additionally, and very importantly for the vendor, there are tax concessions which allow the shares to be treated on the same basis as shares in a private company for Capital Gains Tax and Inheritance Tax purposes.

Simply put, a flotation turns a private company into a public one. In a flotation, a private company, or its shareholders, sell a certain percentage of the company's shares to the public. In return for these shares, the company or its shareholders receive cash. An owner taking his business public has the choice as to how much he will be diluted in terms of ownership. Most owners are interested in maintaining their control position and choose to sell only a minority of their share. Typically a stockbroker is retained to act as agent in placing the shares with the public.

Once your business goes public, you will immediately discover many changes beyond simply the increase in the number of your shareholders. After a flotation, a newly public company must conform with the relevant regulatory, financial and legal requirements. Among other things, the Stock Exchange requires all public companies to publish interim reports on their performance and operations, which become publicly available information. It is through these interim reports that the company communicates with its shareholders and other potential investors.

As an owner of a private company used to disclosing nothing about your business to outsiders, such public reporting will seem disconcerting at first. Competitors and customers alike can access such information as operating margins and labour costs. Most MDs of newly public companies are not prepared for the sudden public availability of their previously private operating data (including your remuneration and service contract which has to be available for inspection). Many owners compare running a public company to 'living in a fishbowl'.

Even more disturbing to owners of private businesses is the cost of obtaining a listing, and then the on-going cost of being a publicly listed company. The initial cost of obtaining a quote on the AIM market can easily be £300,000 (excluding brokers' commissions based on the amount of money raised). Considering fees for on-going stock broker, legal and public relations efforts (plus additional costs for printing and posting of results to all shareholders), the annual cost of being public is likely to be £50,000, and can rise quickly.

For many, if not most, private companies, a flotation is not a viable option. Compared with the many thousands of small to medium-sized private companies, there are fewer than 2,400 publicly listed firms on the Stock Market and Alternative Investment Market. Even in the United States there are only 7,500 firms on the New York Stock Exchange, American Stock Exchange and NASDAQ.

Clearly, the vast majority of private companies are not candidates to 'go public'. For owners facing retirement or succession dilemmas, a flotation is clearly not a viable alternative. Many private companies just do not have sufficient 'critical mass' or are not the type of business that would command interest in the public markets. Yet, for those whose companies have the appropriate characteristics, a flotation can offer tremendous advantages. The most significant advantage is the opportunity to achieve some liquidity for yourself and to raise capital for your business, all without yielding control of your company.

Owners considering a sale need to weigh the relative strengths and weaknesses of a flotation before determining which path to take. Only by seriously considering a flotation can you be certain that the decision to sell is best for you.

Both a flotation and a sale offer significantly different realities for owners of private companies, specifically in the areas of:

- the amount and extent of liquidity you achieve;
- the growth possibilities afforded your company;
- your continued control over operations and strategic planning;
- the stability of the respective markets.

Liquidity

A sale of a business obviously provides you with the most natural path to liquidity. Through a sale, you are able to reclaim your assets from your company and spread them among numerous other, more liquid investments. A sale also eliminates all on-going business risk. Whether you stay on to run the business or not, a sale frees you from the financial concerns of the business. No longer does your net worth rise and fall with the fortunes of your company.

Though some sale transactions involve either a retention of some equity in your business or other on-going contingent payments, a sale typically leaves you with only minor participation in the future growth or success of your company. Whatever 'upside' gains are generated in the future belong to the acquirer.

A flotation, on the other hand, allows you to actively participate in the continued 'upside' of the business. Through a flotation, you may retain significant equity in the future growth of the company. (Of course, the converse is also true: you also share significantly in the 'downside' risk.)

While a flotation provides immediate cash to the business and to you personally, you will continue to hold much of your wealth in company shares, the liquidity and value of which is exposed to business (and stock market) vagaries.

Generally, most companies with smaller market capitalisations and a limited number of shares in public hands find that their shares have little aftermarket float (in other words, they are not traded often enough or in large enough quantity to allow one to sell or buy without dramatically disrupting price). Even for companies with larger market values, the possibility always exists that sufficient secondary markets do not develop for their shares, making it difficult for investors to trade their shares. Investors tend to seek those shares that offer a sense of order and fluidity in trading patterns. For a public company with little 'free float' in its shares, it is quite possible for an owner to have no more liquidity than when he was private.

It is also important to note that with most flotations, significant shareholders will be required by the stockbrokers to agree not to sell their shares for a period of time (known as the 'lock-in' arrangement), thus further dampening the potential liquidity.

To provide continued access to capital for both a company and its shareholders through subsequent share offerings, the MD of a public company must work to ensure that a deep and dependable market exists for his company's shares. The traditional solution to this problem is to go public using a stockbroker with the size, clout and commitment to follow the company after the initial offering. The larger, more established stockbrokers like Peel Hunt and Collins Stevant have analysts to follow and research their clients' shares and stir up interest in their stocks. These stockbrokers act as diligent 'market makers' and provide active aftermarket support.

Growth possibilities

A flotation generates immediate capital to fund your company's growth plans. Often, the greater a company's growth opportunities, the greater its capital needs. If a publicly listed company requires continued funding to exploit new growth opportunities, it will have to return to the public markets to raise additional money. As discussed earlier, subsequent public offerings are conditional on the performance of the company and the market for the shares.

A sale on the other hand can provide continued access to capital through its parent. In addition, a sale can provide greater resources than merely the acquirer's capital. A larger company with the 'right' fit can bring manufacturing and production efficiencies, wider distribution channels, broader marketing capabilities, a share of the administrative and overhead burden, and a greater general stature in the market. The ice-cream maker Haagen-Dazs established an international presence and distribution far quicker and more efficiently under the aegis of Pillsbury than would have been possible had it remained independent. By selling to the 'right' party, a company can position itself to take advantage of its acquirer's strengths to grow at an even quicker pace than it had on its own.

Control

The possibility of retaining an element of control is probably the single greatest advantage of a flotation. Most owners going through a flotation emerge in control of their company. It is this very feature that prompts many business owners to seek an a listing.

In a sale, even if you remain as MD of the company, you will ultimately lose total command over your company. Regardless of promises made by an acquirer or the operating duties retained after a sale, once your business has been sold you transfer ultimate authority to the acquirer. This can be a difficult fact for some owners to accept, especially those remaining in an executive capacity. Rightly or wrongly, no new owner will operate your company exactly as you have. This, of course, can be cause for either resentment or arguments.

While owners who take their business public do generally maintain control, they are still answerable to their public shareholders and the market at large. Most private business owners are not accustomed to operating to the City's short-term standards, being judged solely by interim results.

Indeed, the performance of the shares in the aftermarket is the yardstick by which every public company (and its management) is ultimately measured. Not coincidentally, the performance of the shares also becomes the yardstick by which the MD's net worth is measured. While a MD may 'control' his public company, his fortunes are still subject to the vagaries of the market.

Stability of the markets

There is quite a contrast between the relative stability of the new flotation, or Initial Public Offering market and the acquisition market. In general, the IPO market is significantly more volatile. Over the past two decades, it has not been uncommon for the number of public offerings to jump dramatically from one year to next. Both individual and institutional appetite for IPOs changes rapidly, depending on overall stock market conditions and the liquidity in financial markets. Regardless of your own company's performance and prospects, when the IPO window is closed, it is almost impossible to raise money in the markets.

The number of UK flotations varies widely each year, from 106 in 1998 to 317 in 2000, and dropping down to 103 in 2002. While the merger and acquisition markets have displayed some ebb and flow of activity over the past two decades, the general trend has been more consistent and stable, particularly in the medium-sized transactions. While 2001 and 2002 saw a drop in very large cross-border transactions, the value of sub-£100 million transactions held up well.

Both the IPO and M&A markets are closely tied to the general business and financial markets. However, the IPO market has a far greater tendency to open wide for certain opportunities, only to close abruptly. During periods of peak activity and interest, the IPO market tends to offer higher overall company valuations and greater receptivity to marginal deals. However, it is important for owners to move quickly when the IPO markets are hot, as history has demonstrated that periods of high demand are often quickly followed by periods of great malaise.

The merger market, on the other hand, is more consistent and predictable. Activity and pricing does move up and down with the overall markets, but within relatively narrow bands. The merger market is always open and receptive to good deals, unlike the IPO market. Large strategic buyers are always seeking growth, geographic expansion and new products through acquisitions.

An owner considering going public must keep an eye on the relative strength of the IPO markets in judging the timing of his move. Though the health of the markets is an important consideration in a sale, it is certainly a less crucial factor than in a flotation.

3 *What your company is worth: a question of value*

Just as beauty is in the eye of the beholder, a company's value is determined by the interest it generates in the market. You may believe that your company is worth £20 million, but if the best offer you can get from the market is £10 million, then your company is only worth £10 million.

While there are numerous quantitative methods you can employ to estimate the value of your business, the true value can only be determined by the market. By definition, fair market value is the price that a commodity can bring in an open exchange between knowledgeable buyers and sellers in an unfettered market. Valuations are done in the abstract, transactions in the concrete.

Unless the person preparing the valuation of your company subsequently makes you an offer, the valuation may prove to be meaningless. No valuation study, however exhaustive or detailed, can determine the actual market value of your company. Only buyers can do that. Regardless of the conclusions of any independent analysis and valuation, it takes two parties, a buyer and a seller, to agree on a price, complete a transaction and set a true value on your company.

A company whose securities trade in a public forum benefits from having its value set on a daily basis. Private companies are not so fortunate. There is probably nothing more difficult in finance than placing a value on a company for which no market exists.

By its very nature, a valuation is an estimate of the price that a company could bring in the open market. At its best, a valuation can give you some idea of what range of prices you might expect to realise in the market. However, you need to recognise a valuation for what it is: merely one opinion of the ultimate worth of your business. Valuations are more art than science, and a very imprecise art at that.

A few years ago, we were engaged to sell a Birmingham-based distributor of industrial products. After dutiful quantitative analysis, we concluded that the client's business was worth approximately £12–14 million. After soliciting bids from a number of logical suitors, we were quite dismayed when all of the offers came in around £10 million.

We searched further and were able to locate a large American manufacturer of engineered parts that was interested in expanding its distribution to Britain. To our astonishment, the American firm came in with an initial offer of £16 million. Obviously, the Americans rationalised their offer by how well our client fitted in with their own strategic plans. It was clearly cheaper to acquire our client than to incur the cost of starting their own operation and suffering through several years of losses. The acquisition would also have the additional benefit of eliminating one of their potential competitors. We were eventually able to negotiate the American company up to £17 million, a deal that is still talked about in the industry today.

Just as our valuation model overestimated the offers we expected to generate from the domestic bidders, it significantly underestimated the value the American group saw in the business. There was no way to justify this differential using common valuation techniques. The Americans were not employing our valuation methods; they obviously viewed this deal from quite a different perspective.

Before going to market, you should first go through the process of estimating a range of potential values for your business. Even assuming their inherent limitations, valuation studies can none the less provide you with some general indications as to what prices might be both realistic and realizable. It is always advisable to have a complete and detailed understanding of possible values at the outset, so selling shareholders and advisers alike are clear as to expectations and realistic goals.

(In understanding the concepts presented in this chapter, it is important to recognise that value is being defined in terms of cash or cash equivalents. It is clear that £10 million in cash value is not equal to £10 million in a 4 per cent, 20-year, unsecured loan note. In describing various methods of estimating a company's value, we are generally talking about its cash value, or 'present value' in merger parlance.)

Over the years, certain methods of valuation have come to be accepted by professionals in the merger industry. While literally dozens of different quantitative approaches have been developed, you should only focus on those methods that are commonly employed by buyers and lenders in the market. After all, by using the same methods, you and your suitors will at least be approaching the question of value from the same perspective. You may not agree with buyers on either their assumptions or their conclusions, but at least you can negotiate and argue from a common ground.

There is no single factor on which value hinges. Value is ultimately determined by a combination of numerous elements, including a company's assets, its past performance, its future earnings prospects, the outlook of its industry and geographic market, and the strength of such intangibles as management and products.

Each potential acquirer will look at your company from a different vantage point, with differing motivations as to why they want to buy your company. Some suitors may be seeking to broaden their markets; others may be looking to bring manufacturing capabilities in-house. Still others may simply be looking for new opportunities in which to invest their cash.

Every acquirer will have their own, internal methods of valuing your business. Depending on such factors as their cost of money, potential operating synergies or alternative opportunities, each acquirer will develop their own, unique perspective on the value of your company.

Methods of valuation

Three fundamental methods of valuation have come to be commonly accepted in the merger field:

1. the underlying asset value;
2. the multiple of income basis;
3. the discounted cash flow basis.

Although these methods vary in their applicability, depending on specific facts or circumstances, they do at least indicate a range of values based on certain commonly accepted fundamentals and principles. By analysing the values indicated by each of these three methods, coupled with an understanding of current market conditions, you can form an objective opinion as to the fair value of your company. The three basic approaches to valuation are defined below.

1. Underlying asset value

In the asset approach, the underlying tangible assets of an enterprise are considered individually. The sum of the fair values of each asset, after netting out the aggregate total of the company's tangible liabilities, represents the asset value of a company.

There are a number of different derivations of asset-based valuations; they can be based on liquidation value, replacement cost value or fair market value. Of these, fair market value is generally considered the most appropriate.

'Book value' (or the original cost of the assets minus the depreciation charged to date) should not be a consideration. Book value is not really a definition of value, but rather an accounting concept fraught with the vagaries of differing depreciation methods and accounting policies. Book value represents the historic cost of a company's assets, not their market values. All the company's assets can easily be adjusted to market value, however, by considering such obvious factors as excess depreciation, stock provisions or 'cushions' and unstated assets, as well as updated appraisals of fixed assets.

The asset approach is generally considered most appropriate for companies with significant tangible assets, such as property holding companies or natural resource companies. Asset-based valuations are also germane for those companies that do not generate an acceptable return on their assets. Such companies are often worth more dead than alive, and are usually sold for their asset values prior to being liquidated.

Owners of profitable companies generally assume that asset-based valuations are not suitable for their situations. These owners tend to believe that their companies should be valued on their profitability, market presence and other intangible benefits, not merely the worth of their tangible assets. There is certainly some logic to this argument. Most valuation studies do indeed emphasise the profitability (or anticipated profitability) of the subject companies. The difference between the value of the underlying assets and the business value is goodwill.

No valuation, however, can ignore the question of a company's underlying assets. Value is always based on an interplay between a company's assets and its profits. While profits (or potential profits) may be the more salient factor in determining value, buyers tend to 'shy away' from a deal that involves too few assets and too much goodwill. Thus, each buyer will examine your asset base in great detail before determining an acceptable value. Everything else being equal, a company that can deliver a higher asset value is worth more, primarily because the transaction generates less goodwill for the buyer. ('Goodwill' is explained in greater detail in Chapter 7.)

2. Multiple of income basis

The multiple of income basis compares your company's operations and financial performance with that of 1) similar publicly traded companies and 2) recent sale transactions involving like private companies. Since you are estimating the value of your company for acquisition purposes, the merger markets will generally provide a more accurate benchmark than a comparison with publicly traded companies.

The market comparison approach is similar to the methodology used in the property market. By looking at transactions involving other like properties, you can generate a good understanding of the range of values in which your property should trade.

A full comparative analysis examines such factors as: price/earnings ratios, price/book value ratios, price/sales ratios, debt-to-equity ratios, return on sales (profits/sales), return on assets (profits/assets), and return on equity (profits/shareholders' equity). Of these, the most broadly used comparative measure is the price/earnings (P/E) ratio. For private companies, this ratio generally represents the indicated price (or value) over the current profit (after taxes and interest), and is expressed as a multiple of earnings. You must ensure that all parties are calculating this on the same basis, ie before or after tax. Some calculate the multiple on a before tax profit. With Corporation Tax at 30 per cent the resultant ratio is considerably different. A P/E ratio (post tax) of 10 per cent is the same as on earnings multiple (pre tax) of 7.

P/E multiples are used to gauge broad investor sentiment towards the economy in general and your industry and company in particular. Companies that offer above-average growth possibilities tend to command higher P/E multiples. Conversely, companies that operate in mundane industries or offer little in the way of growth opportunities generally trade at low P/Es.

If a comparative analysis finds that companies broadly similar to yours tend to sell for 5–7 times current operating earnings, then you might safely assume that acquirers would expect to pay the same for your company. If, however, your company operates at a 40 per cent gross margin versus the industry average of 30 per cent, then you may well be able to justify a premium to the comparative industry average, based on your superior operating capabilities. By comparing your operating ratios with the comparative 'peer' group, you will be able to make a subjective determination of where in the range of pricing ratios your company should trade.

A P/E ratio can also be expressed in its inverse form, called the capitalisation rate (a multiple of 5 corresponds to a 20 per cent capitalisation rate). The capitalisation rate represents an annualised return an investor should expect (or demand) from his investment.

UK Treasury Notes or other sovereign governmental obligations are defined by the market as being 'riskless' investments. If Treasuries are yielding 6–7 per cent, most investors or acquirers will demand a premium over that return to be 'induced' to make another, riskier investment. Because most smaller, private companies represent risky, illiquid investments, most acquirers of private companies seek a 15–30 per cent return on their investments, to compensate them with an appropriate 'premium'.

Thus, buyers have to be convinced that significant growth possibilities exist for them to pay a high multiple for your business. After all, a multiple of 10 times operating earnings implies only a 10 per cent pre-tax return on investment, just a slight premium to the 'riskless' return of Treasury Notes. No rational investor or acquirer would make that investment unless he was convinced that earnings could grow dramatically. Indeed, assuming a multiple of 10 times operating income, earnings would have to grow at a compound rate of 25 per cent over five years to provide the minimum 20 per cent annualised return on investment.

Comparisons are sometimes easier said than done. It is important to choose a universe of comparative companies that are similar in size, capitalisation and industry. The problem is that the companies most like yours are typically other private companies, for which little or no public data exists. The same is true for sale transactions involving comparable private companies.

It is important to be very selective in comparing your operations with those of public companies. While data on these companies is readily available, most public companies will tend to be larger and more diversified than your own business. Markets tend to reward larger companies with higher multiples – primarily because they tend to have a breadth of products and a certain 'critical mass' that eludes most smaller, private companies. It is totally inappropriate for an owner of a £25 million manufacturer of test instruments to compare his operations with those of Hewlett-Packard.

In every comparison, you must be certain that you have enough facts on each company and its operations to make a sound judgement. For instance, you may know that your competitor sold for £15 million. But without any more information than that, you are in no position to judge your own comparative value. Your competitor's business may have been more profitable than yours, it may have had a larger asset base or it may have had a significantly higher return on equity. Without a full understanding of those companies in your comparative universe, you must be somewhat wary of whatever conclusions result.

Value is always determined in the margin. If your neighbour's house recently sold for £250,000, everyone in your street will immediately adjust their internal expectations as to the value of their own house. However, if everyone in your street suddenly put their house up for sale at the same time, prices would plunge from the weight of too much supply. Thus, it is the marginal deal, the last incremental deal, that sets value expectations for all.

Over the past two decades, small to mid-sized private companies have tended to trade in the range of 4–8 times current year adjusted operating profits. In slow or difficult markets, the range has slid lower; in hot markets, the range has moved slightly higher. While the great majority of middle market deals are completed in this range, a good quarter of all deals trade higher or lower.

The multiple of income basis assumes that a few recent deals are appropriate indicators of value. This may not always be the case. We recently sold a distributor of hydraulic components to a well-funded private equity group that was looking to consolidate in the field. The buyer paid a very high price for our client, as a cost of entry into the market. Once the group had purchased this company, however, they had established their presence in that region and were only interested in acquiring any other companies as 'add-on' acquisitions at substantially lower multiples. Thus, other distributors of hydraulic components may have wrongly used that transaction as a model of what value they could expect. Firms often pay 'premiums' to gain a foothold in a field, setting standards that no other parties in the field will subsequently match.

3. Discounted cash flow method (DCF)

The discounted cash flow method is based on the present worth of the future economic benefits to be derived by an acquirer. This approach attempts to determine the net present value of a company's expected future earnings stream over a certain 'payback' period. This method requires projections of future profits, based primarily on past results and assumptions as to future operating performance. These figures are then discounted back to a present value, using a discount rate competitive with rates of investments of comparable risk. (A discount rate is a rate at which annual future earnings are discounted to reflect the effects of inflation, the cost of money and the inherent risk of an investment.)

Most prospective buyers will tend to use some form of this model in assessing the value of your company. They will make their own judgements as to your future prospects and try to quantify those assessments into a set of projections. Most acquirers incorporate such factors as anticipated cost savings, synergies and new product development into their models. Obviously, these figures are never known by the seller.

The difficulty in preparing an discounted cash flow method is arriving at good, credible projections that all parties can live with. Sellers tend to be overly optimistic; buyers tend to be overly cautious. Buyers always believe that projections provided by sellers are suspect.

This method also involves important and often difficult judgements with regard to growth assumptions, cost savings, and the discount rate applied. Merger specialists have developed rather elaborate models to help you refine key variables in your projections, such as working capital needs and variable costs.

The strength of the discounted cash flow method is that it examines your business the way most prospective buyers will: it looks to the future rather than to the past. The weakness is that its reliability depends on the quality and credibility of the projections.

Profits

While the final determinate of your company's value may rest on a number of variables, your company's current and anticipated profits stream is clearly the most important factor driving value. When an acquirer is willing to pay a 'premium' for your company, it is generally based on the assumption that your earnings will grow at above-market rates, either through efficiencies or synergies that the buyer brings to the deal.

The key to the value of most businesses is the ability to generate earnings. And yet, in order to minimise income taxes, many private company owners seek to suppress reported profits. Typical methods employed by owners to reduce taxable earnings include: generating inventory 'cushions' to minimise gross profits, expensing costs that should appropriately be capitalised, delaying the recognition of revenues into the next financial year, and expensing personal entertainment, meal, travel, vehicle and insurance costs through their companies. In addition, many owners draw a salary well in excess of what an outsider might term 'reasonable'. Thus, the financial statements of most private companies do not reflect the full profitability of these businesses.

In order to provide a true economic view of these companies, it is imperative to adjust their financial statements to eliminate direct and indirect owner-related expenses, as well as expenses of an extraordinary, discretionary or non-recurring nature.

Because you want to identify all of the areas of potential profit enhancement, it is advisable to go through your profit and loss account on a line-by-line basis. One client of ours reported negligible profits, and at first sight it did not look like a very good candidate for sale. But when we started looking into the figures, it soon became obvious that the owner enjoyed a very good income and lifestyle from the company. Our client put all his personal expenditure through the company, including a salary in excess of £500,000, pension contributions of over £100,000, salaries to wife and mother, a host of vehicles including a Rolls-Royce, Porsche Turbo and Range Rover, a boat and a villa. The total of these added up to costs in the profit and loss account approaching £1 million. Once we had rewritten the accounts for the past three years, a very different view was taken about the profitability and value of the company.

Most sophisticated acquirers will understand and accept the concept of re-stating your financial statements to reflect the 'true' profitability of your company. However, you will probably run into arguments over the extent and nature of some of your 'add-backs'. First, buyers only recognise those add-backs that can be identified and documented; they will generally not accept those items that cannot be proven, such as hidden stock or diverted cash. In addition, what you consider an unusual or 'non-recurring' expense may elicit a different response from a buyer. Professional fees and marketing costs are a normal, on-going part of doing business. Depreciation, too, is a legitimate cost of being in business, except in instances where depreciation costs are well above anticipated future capital expenditures (after all, you will eventually need to replace or upgrade your plant and equipment).

You should add-back to company income only that portion of directors' salaries that is excessive, not the entire amount. After all, someone has to be paid to run the business.

Lastly, buyers will generally not pay you for efficiencies or synergies they bring to the table. Many sellers attempt to reconstruct their Profit/ Loss statements based on what costs could be eliminated by combining with a prospective buyer. While these efficiencies or synergies may be very real, it is rare that a buyer will pay you for what they bring to a deal. In most transactions, buyers value your business as a 'stand-alone' operation. Whatever efficiencies that accrue from a deal generally belong to the buyer.

Myths about value

Ignoring conventional methods of valuation, many owners base their 'asking price' on a number of myths and misconceptions about value. A few are outlined below.

1. The labour theory of value

Karl Marx developed this specious concept over 150 years ago. Some business owners would be horrified to know that they are unknowingly perpetuating it today.

In essence, the labour theory of value claims that a commodity's value should be based on the amount of labour that goes into producing it. Many owners wrongly believe that the value of their company should be directly related to the amount of work that they put into it. They tell us that they deserve a high price because of all of the sweat and toil they endured over the years.

This argument is akin to an artist who insists that his paintings should command high prices because he has spent years creating them. His art may fetch a high price, or it may not. Buyers will clearly value the art based on their own criteria, not by how much time the artist spent creating it.

The value of your business is independent of the many years you spent building it. The free enterprise system is based on market forces determining value, not labour content. Markets reward competence and creativity as evidenced by profits (or anticipated profits). The years it took to build your company is an irrelevant matter.

2. The revenue theory of value

Some owners suggest that extraordinary growth rates should command above-market values. That may be the case, but only if the growth is achieved with a commensurate increase in profitability.

It is not particularly impressive to grow sales at the expense of margins and profitability. The key is to grow sales profitably. Buyers tend to focus on the bottom line, not the top line. After all, you are generally paid multiples of earnings, not revenues.

3. The 'Just gimme my price' theory of value

A few owners ignore convention entirely and base their valuation assumptions on something more immediate: what they want to net from a deal. Regardless of the inherent strengths or weaknesses of their company, these owners start the valuation process by first determining what they want from a deal, and then work backwards to justify that number.

A recent client demanded that his business be sold for £12 million, not based on any analytical study of the inherent merits of his company, but because he wanted to leave a certain amount to each of his children. This client actually spurned numerous offers of £9–10 million, even though those offers were presented with sound price justifications. To our knowledge, the company is still on the market, and now worth about £6 million, as the market is past its peak. Businesses are valued on their inherent strengths and weaknesses, not an owner's whimsical desire to support his lifestyle or that of his progeny.

Conclusion

Too many owners place an unrealistically high value on their business, because of either emotional attachments or a non-objective assessment of their company. In the end, you only wind up hurting yourself with unrealistic or insupportable expectations. Potential suitors may not even consider buying your business if they assume that a high asking price means that you are not serious about selling. Premium prices are occasionally paid for businesses, but you should never go through the time and effort of marketing your business expecting such a premium.

As we stated earlier, it is important that you establish value goals prior to marketing your company, if only to frame your reference of expectations. However, you need to keep in mind that this is only a starting point. Value is ephemeral; it is based on perception as much as fact. Many variables beyond the hard numbers will impact the eventual value of your business, including such intangible factors as your strengths, weaknesses and prospects, as well as the buyer's ultimate objectives.

We never give an asking price to purchasers, we simple ask them to offer 'what it is worth to them'. In this way, we do not put them off by asking too much, nor do we lower expectations for the strategic buyer. Value, like beauty, is in the eye of the beholder.

4   *Issues to address before considering a sale*

Once you have made a decision to sell, there are a number of preparatory actions you should take in order to make your company more attractive to potential buyers. Just as home-owners often remodel or repaint their house to help them sell, business owners should take similar steps in preparing their company for the market. As is true with most things in life, planning pays. By working through the following checklist of 'housekeeping chores', you will set the proper stage on which to market your company to outside parties. In addition, you may well significantly enhance the value of your business.

Initial impressions are very important in attracting and retaining the interest of potential suitors. Most of the actions that we outline in this chapter are aimed at satisfying prospective buyers' initial concerns, to make them comfortable enough to take a closer look. Over time, many companies develop policies and characteristics that are confusing or incomprehensible to others. It is difficult enough to convince potential acquirers to pay a premium price for your company; you need to help the process along by making your company as inviting and understandable as possible.

The 'housekeeping chores' that we suggest may take from two to 12 months to implement. In the end, however, the effort will be rewarded by the increased interest and value you will get for your company. As an aside, all of these actions are good business practice and will help you to better manage and develop the business, even if you never sell.

Position your financial statements to your advantage

The first place to start a programme of examination and correction is in the area of finance. After all, most decisions relating to value ultimately boil down to the past and potential earning power of your company. Thus, in contemplating a sale, it is vitally important that you first address how you can strengthen or better document your company's financial health.

Straighten out your financial affairs

Many private businesses are run more like sole proprietorships than public companies. Indeed, many owners operate their companies not to produce a stellar profit and loss account for shareholders, but rather for their own personal benefit.

Most acquirers understand owners' desires to minimise taxable income. They accept many of the techniques owners employ to mask their earnings, such as accelerated depreciation, delaying recognition of revenue, expensing capital outlays, excessive remuneration and owner perks. However, there are quite a number of tax-avoidance schemes that are of such a nature that they will 'turn off' prospective buyers. For example, owners of companies with a large 'cash' business can often divert some of the discretionary cash from the company straight into their own pockets. Alternatively, through the use of 'inventory cushions', or the deliberate undervaluing of stock, owners are able to hide their profits from the taxman. You should not underestimate the negative impact of such questionable behaviour on a potential acquirer. *Some* buyers will walk away from a deal at the first sight of such illegal or unethical acts. *All* buyers will require you to indemnify them from any tax problems arising from your actions.

You should also be aware that such deliberate attempts to escape taxes may cause more than ethical dilemmas. Buyers will typically only recognise a company's traceable reconstructed profits; they will not pay for earnings that are not easily or clearly documented. Owners who have become adept at hiding profits from the tax authorities have the perverse challenge of having to prove to potential acquirers that those profits ever existed. Some owners have devised tax-avoidance schemes so complex that they can hardly recreate themselves what they did, let alone explain their actions to a prospective suitor.

The most direct way to deal with this dilemma is to 'invest in taxes' for a year or two. To prove that profits exist, you need to show them. Yes, this means that taxes will have to be paid (a horrible thought to some owners). But, given the fact that businesses are bought on a multiple of earnings, the investment of one year's taxes should reap multiples of that sum in a sale.

Likewise, you need to address the miscellaneous financial aspects of your business that have no direct bearing on your company's operations. If you have personal property or equipment on your company's books, or there are corporate assets you want to keep after the sale, like a large tract of undeveloped land adjacent to a factory, you should buy them or distribute them before you go to market. Their presence will just complicate and confuse matters later on.

Shareholder loans or inter-company receivables should be cleared up. Again, you do not want to make your balance sheet any more complicated than necessary.

You should also consider spinning off or eliminating marginal operations or subsidiary operations that are not central to your core business. We once worked with a client in the plastics-moulding business. The company also owned a small car-wash adjacent to one of its factories. Though the owner loved his car-wash, it was clearly not germane to his plastics business. Potential buyers of his plastics company had no interest in also buying the car-wash. After several failed negotiations, we finally advised the client to spin off the car-wash to himself, in order to make a deal for the plastics company more palatable for suitors.

While this example may appear extreme, it certainly makes sense to remove from the buyer's consideration any unrelated businesses or assets, primarily so you do not steer the focus away from the core company.

Get audited statements

Having your financial statements audited, especially by one of the recognised accounting firms, increases a prospective buyer's faith in your company's financial position. Regardless of the terms of the deal, most prospective acquirers will carry out financial due diligence prior to buying your company. By providing potential suitors with audited accounts at the outset, you accelerate the process and clear away one of the inevitable delays leading to completion.

More importantly, by supplying suitors with audited numbers, you indicate your confidence that your figures are accurate and complete. Quite a number of very active buyers in today's marketplace, especially those that are public, refuse to consider any acquisition candidates that do not provide at least three years of audited statements.

You should be aware that an audit should uncover most games that owners play to mask profits. An arm's length financial audit will quickly shed light on profit-avoiding schemes such as excess stock provision. Thus, an audit should force an owner to 'clean up his act', at least in terms of financial reporting. As we mentioned earlier, this may well prove to be beneficial in the increased confidence it gives the buyer.

Clean up your stock and debtors

Over the course of a company's operating history, many owners become lax in policing their stock and debtors. Debtors that have little chance of being collected are still carried at their original value. Stock that is slow-moving or obsolete is not sufficiently marked down. We once had a client who insisted on carrying at full value a customised packaging job he had performed for a company long since bankrupt. Our client sincerely believed that some different customer would one day come calling for that precise job, and he would unload it all at full value.

Prior to buying your company, a prospective acquirer will send in his auditor to ferret out these problems. Most buyers will subtract any debtor or stock problems from the purchase price, essentially giving you nothing for these assets. It makes more sense for you to address these problems yourself. That way, you have the time to either sort out the problems and salvage some value, or write them off and at least take the tax deduction for yourself.

Polish your physical plant

While acquirers are primarily interested in the earnings power of your company, it is important to remember that you are also selling your physical assets. The condition of those physical assets says a tremendous amount about how you run your company and will definitely have an impact on any buyer's impression of your business. A cramped, run-down factory in a seedy part of town could by itself turn away prospective acquirers, even if your company mints money.

It benefits you to spend some time, effort and expense in making your physical plant as clean and presentable as possible prior to showing it to potential suitors. Specifically, you should carry out an inspection and effect any significant repairs or improvements that may be necessary, including:

- painting the exterior and interior walls;
- repairing or replacing all outmoded machinery or equipment;
- performing preventive maintenance on all other machinery and equipment;
- repairing road surfaces, clearing away rubble, and having the landscaping well-maintained;
- cleaning out the office, discarding all unnecessary papers and records that have accumulated;
- sprucing up or reconfiguring the offices to convey a warm, productive and efficient working environment.

No one expects your factory floor to be spotless; you obviously have to continue operating your business throughout the sale process. Some businesses tend to be cleaner than others; most suitors recognise that fact. However, a clean and crisp outward appearance displays both your and your employees' pride in your organisation, and can have a favourable impact on prospective buyers.

A more vexing dilemma involves what to do if you are in dire need of a larger facility, a major piece of equipment or a new computer system. The decision whether to proceed with these projects before selling or to leave those expenditures and headaches to the acquirer is not an easy one. In the end, it will boil down to a question of your desire to spend both the money and the effort to accomplish these tasks versus the incremental value these moves will add to your company.

Quite a number of business owners can clearly see significant benefits in expanding their capacity, but choose not to do so because they just do not want the hassle. On the other hand, we recently represented a distributor of electronic parts who clearly added significant value to his business by patiently waiting through the design, installation and debugging of a sophisticated stock control system.

If you do decide to proceed with a major expansion of your plant or computer system, you must be committed to seeing the project through to completion prior to selling. A company in the midst of a major plant renovation will appear too messy and uncertain a situation for most acquirers. To get any benefit from the time and expenditure involved, you must have both completed the expansion and operated smoothly for some period of time to demonstrate the tangible benefits of the expenditure.

Codify and strengthen legal and contractual affairs

We once worked with a company that had a tradition of signing one-year fixed-term employment contracts with its staff every April Fool's Day. This tradition had been started by the former owner, who had a sense of humour about such things. The policy remained intact when the business was passed down to his son. While longer employment contracts might have been more sensible, each side seemed comfortable with the arrangement. There appeared to be no reason to change.

In fact, there was a very good reason to change: acquirers will most probably view such arrangements with disdain. It is very important to codify any contractual relationships your business has with outside parties. These relationships are a large part of what any acquirer is seeking; every buyer will want assurance as to some predictability and permanence of these relationships.

The most obvious relationships that need to be addressed are leases on plant and equipment, and employment contracts. Acquirers are interested in maintaining operating costs comparable to your present costs. You should try to negotiate long-term leases or contracts at or near historic costs; otherwise, acquirers may use the spectre of an increase in costs as a reason to justify a lower price.

It is unwise to consider selling just before a contract expires. If the pending renegotiation does not frighten away a prospective buyer, the fear of the unknown liability will certainly dampen his enthusiasm and therefore his price. Better to negotiate the contract yourself and provide the acquirer with predictable, known future costs.

Other considerations you should address are any formal contracts or informal relationships you have with suppliers, customers or employees. If your company receives priority pricing from a supplier, or enjoys a special relationship with a customer, it would benefit you to develop these situations into contractual affairs.

It is always advisable to codify and formalise 'terms and conditions' with suppliers and customers, and service contracts for key employees. A major concern of all potential acquirers will be that these relationships will end once they have bought the company and you have left.

Straighten out your records

Private business owners are notoriously poor at maintaining organised business records. Perhaps it is the lack of the discipline of a public market and its various regulatory bodies. Or perhaps it is simply that owners see a greater use of their time in running their business than overseeing adequate record keeping.

Whatever the reason, it is imperative that you develop an accurate and complete accounting of all your business records prior to going to the market. Any potential acquirer will need to examine complete corporate records. It is certainly the sign of a well-disciplined, well-organised company to have its data available at the outset.

As a minimum, you should address the following areas of record keeping:

- articles of incorporation and minutes of directors' and shareholders' meetings;
- all documentation relating to compliance with various governmental regulations, including employees' contracts, pension schemes, health and safety, environmental and equal opportunity matters;
- tax records – you should be certain that you are not behind with any corporate tax returns;
- property leases and contracts binding the company – all should be executed and current;

- payroll records;
- documentation relating to patents, trademarks, or copyrights;
- documentation relating to distribution agreements, representation agreements, licensing agreements or franchise agreements;
- documentation relating to all mortgages, bank loans, hire purchase and lease agreements.

Build a management team for transition

The single greatest asset that your company has is its people. Your hard assets do not generate earnings or market share; rather, your employees do. Therefore, potential acquirers want to know that the same people who developed your company for you will remain to run it for them.

A buyer's greatest fear is that the owner of a business flees town just after his business was acquired, leaving the buyer high and dry. It is imperative that you take the time to develop an experienced and dedicated management team before approaching suitors. Buyers not only want a commitment from an owner to remain for at least a transitional period, but they also like to see a competent second-tier of management, capable of one day assuming control. Buyers want to be made confident that the company can survive its owner.

Businesses that solely revolve around the abilities of their owners are very vulnerable. As far as possible, you should delegate responsibilities and decisions to subordinates, developing a broader base of abilities and experience within the company. The appearance of a phalanx of assertive, capable and dedicated managers anxious to grow the business will make your company much more attractive to buyers.

Establish adequate systems and controls

The presence of adequate information systems and financial controls can have a significant impact on the value of your company. Buyers are often quite willing to pay premiums for companies that have gone through the painful process of establishing sophisticated systems and controls. Not only can these companies provide quick responses to informational needs, but the buyers know that the information will be good, reliable data. In today's fast-changing business climate, the quick availability of reliable information is considered a necessary advantage.

More likely than not, you are not the best one to judge your internal systems and controls. Have your accounting firm, or better yet an outside consultant, review your computer systems and financial controls to make certain that they are consistent with your needs. You may well find the cost and effort of updating your systems are repaid many times over.

Address environmental problems

It is not at all uncommon for businesses today to be operating in violation of various national or local environmental regulations. From the use of an old underground oil tank to the disposal of caustic chemicals into a septic system, many businesses have policies or practices that need to be addressed. Unfortunately, many business owners are probably not even aware that their businesses are in violation of these regulations.

Because environmental problems can be so costly to clean up and because governing agencies are becoming increasing diligent in policing violators, quite a number of buyers today are demanding environmental audits prior to making acquisitions. Even the slightest problem can frighten away the most determined buyer, for fear that other, unknown liabilities exist.

You should take the time to carefully and systematically examine your production processes and facilities. You might engage a qualified site inspector to give you his own assessment as to your environmental health.

We recently represented a client whose sale was delayed by five months while the copper that was found in the soil surrounding his factory was removed. Unbeknownst to the seller, the plant had been used during the First World War as a munitions factory. The copper was left over from the production of bullets! Needless to say, the prospective acquirer was quite upset by this late discovery, and its presence seriously threatened the deal. While the copper in the soil caused no threat to the environment, the regulatory authorities required that it be thoroughly removed before the transaction went through. Some foresight in discovering and cleaning up the soil before negotiations began would have led to a far smoother transaction.

Having your own environmental audit prior to going to market allows you plenty of time both to locate actual or potential problems and to address the problems in the most cost-effective and efficient way. Most acquirers will want you to warrant that there are no environmental problems. If you have taken the time to inspect and fix the problems yourself, you will be in a far better position to do so.

Confront pension issues

One of the most challenging hurdles between a seller and a completed deal can be an under-funded pension scheme. Recently more deals have been delayed, or even terminated, because of an under-funded pension liability than for any other reason.

By their nature, money purchase schemes do not tend to generate problems with under-funding. Final salary schemes, however, set alarm bells ringing for most potential acquirers. A dependence on ever-rising stock market values, together with longer life expectancies, has meant that many final salary schemes have been left under-funded for their ultimate actuarial obligations. This under-funding is a liability of the company.

If your company has a final salary scheme, it is imperative that you employ a reputable actuary to determine the current value of the pension scheme and the extent, if any, of its under-funding. By confronting these issues before going to market, you leave yourself time and flexibility in how you might address the potential liability.

Any acquirer will insist on an up-to-date actuarial report, often from an independent actuary. Not only does this report take time to complete, but frequently your actuary and the purchaser's actuary will disagree to the quantum of liabilities.

Ultimately any under-funding is a liability of your company, and will be netted from your gross proceeds. It is best to take the time and effort to address any under-funding in the most efficient and effective manner you can before engaging any suitor in discussions.

Conclusion

To summarise: the key to preparing your business for sale is to look at your company from the perspective of the buyer and ask yourself 'If I were buying this company, what would worry me?' Once you have honestly answered the question, take the necessary steps to remedy the situation. By going through such an introspective exercise, you will be well on your way to making your business more attractive to others.

5

How advisers fit into the picture

In building your company, you have undoubtedly made invaluable contacts within your industry. Most probably you have also had numerous occasions to develop your negotiating skills, perhaps in acquiring one or more companies yourself. Thus, you would probably not be surprised that many business owners decide to sell their business by themselves. Yet, as the old saying goes, a doctor who performs surgery on himself has a fool for a patient. Our experience shows that the same can be said about a business owner who attempts to sell his own business.

Selling a business can be a very complex and time-consuming proposition. There are many legal, tax, accounting and regulatory issues to address. In addition, there is the matter of finding the appropriate buyer for your company, and then negotiating and structuring the most advantageous deal for yourself.

The sale of your business could well be the most important economic decision you make. To help you arrange the best transaction for your needs, you should consider using a qualified professional corporate finance adviser to guide you through the sale process. After all, the cost of good advice is cheap compared to the cost of a serious error of judgement.

The corporate finance adviser (sometimes an investment banker for larger £100 million-plus deals) is essentially an agent authorised to act for you in arranging and negotiating a transaction. Advisers can act for either buyers or sellers; often, both sides of a deal will engage their own advisers. The basic role of an adviser is to search for appropriate acquisition candidates for his client and then negotiate and structure a deal. An adviser works with his client throughout the sale process, from devising the initial strategy to seeing the transaction through to completion. It is important to note that while an adviser represents his client's interests in the market, he is not in a legal position to commit his client to anything.

Corporate finance advisers are not to be confused with brokers or finders, whose main purpose is to introduce two parties in the hope of creating a deal, for which a fee is paid. Brokers generally play a limited role in any transaction; they are not representatives for one side or the other. Rather, they are working for the 'deal'. Brokers simply bring two parties together with the idea of fostering a transaction.

Leaving brokers aside, there are many reasons to use an adviser in selling your business, including the following.

Experience

It has taken you years to develop the skills necessary to build a successful company. Likewise, a competent adviser has spent years developing an understanding of and experience in the field of mergers and acquisitions. A professional adviser brings to a transaction an intimate knowledge of both the current market and the acquisition process, and can help you to properly value and package your company. A competent adviser also has the skills necessary to handle the technical aspects of a sale, including structuring a transaction to meet your objectives and advising on evolving tax, legal, accounting and regulatory issues.

Objectivity

Company owners often have a large emotional stake in their business, which hinders their objectivity in both valuing their company and negotiating the sale transaction. It is difficult for an owner to separate himself from his emotions in selling his business. Better to let an adviser represent your interests in the market, if nothing more than to provide an independent perspective on the process.

Grant Thornton Corporate Finance,
specialists in selling mid-market...

Grant Thornton ⬢

...companies and entrepreneurial businesses. Our dedicated teams have extensive experience across many industries and understand the commercial and emotional issues involved throughout the sale process.

Through robust, independent advice we help vendors by:

- grooming their business for sale
- minimising the tax burden
- compiling an information memorandum for prospective buyers
- identifying and targeting the right buyers
- negotiating the best terms for the deal
- driving the deal to completion.

Visit our dedicated website **www.companiesforsale.uk.com** or call **Andrew Roberts**, Partner and National Head of Disposals on **T** 0121 232 5210 for a confidential discussion.

"The sale of Risk Waters was far more complex than envisaged but **Grant Thornton Corporate Finance delivered**"...

Grant Thornton 🦘

"The Grant Thornton team were instrumental in making the sale of Pete Osborne Logistics happen. Yes **their expertise was crucial** to the success of the deal...

Grant Thornton 🐚

...but they also brought a practical, 'roll the sleeves up' approach to the process, giving constant support as the deal evolved. In short, they made sure that a deal was delivered for the benefit of all concerned."

Pete Osborne
Founder of Pete Osborne Logistics

Pete Osborne Logistics has been acquired by the Stiller Group, with the vendors being advised by Grant Thornton Corporate Finance. Pete Osborne Logistics, based in Darton, South Yorkshire, provides integrated logistic solutions consisting of road haulage and warehousing.

Stiller Group, based in Stockton-on-Tees, provides quality led transport and distribution solutions covering a wide range of sectors from chemicals to steel and consumer goods to commercial waste.

Commenting on the deal Jonathan Shipton, Senior Manager at Grant Thornton Corporate Finance said, "The expertise Pete Osborne Logistics has in integrated solutions complements Stiller's already diverse service offering. The combination of these two businesses will bring significant benefits to clients of the enlarged group."

"This transaction has demonstrated that in spite of challenging market conditions, with a willingness on the part of both vendors and purchasers, deal activity in the transport sector will continue."

For more information contact:
Jonathan Shipton
Grant Thornton
St John's Centre
110 Albion Street
Leeds LS2 8LA
T 0113 209 5255
E jonathan.shipton@gtuk.com
W www.grant-thornton.co.uk
W www.companiesforsale.uk.com

Knowledge of buyers

You may believe that you already know your likely acquirers: your competitors. Yet frequently, much higher values come from buyers outside your specific industry. An adviser can provide your company with exposure to a much broader range of potential suitors, including foreign multinational firms, large and small domestic companies and private investor groups. Because of their stature in the market and their experience, merger advisers can often get better access to corporate officers and key 'decision makers' than you can yourself.

Confidentiality

Most owners contemplating a sale want to be certain that the matter is handled as discreetly and confidentially as possible. A leak to key employees, customers or suppliers could cause a significant disruption of business. In general, the more direct the contact between you and potential acquirers, the greater the chance that the confidentiality of the project will be violated.

It is the role of an adviser to initiate and maintain all contact with potential acquirers. By orchestrating and controlling the sale from a remote site, an adviser insulates you from any direct exposure to buyers until the proper time. Through judicious screening of buyers and the use of strong confidentiality agreements, a competent adviser should be able to maintain confidentiality throughout the sale process.

Skill at negotiations

More likely than not, the eventual buyer of your business will have been through the acquisition process numerous times before encountering you. You, on the other hand, probably have limited experience in such matters. Thus it is vitally important that you have an expert in your corner, not only to negotiate the best terms, but to structure the transaction so that it meets your personal, financial and corporate needs. Because an adviser has no legal authority to commit on your behalf, he can actually give you an advantage, always having to check with you before agreeing to anything. This allows you to preserve your flexibility and gives you the 'upper hand' in negotiations. The evolving laws regarding tax, accounting and estate planning issues are another prime reason to engage an expert to guide you through this complex maze.

Role as a buffer

Because a buyer and seller often end up working together in some form after the acquisition, it is important to develop and maintain a positive relationship throughout the sale process. Yet this is often difficult to do when the two principals are negotiating for themselves. An adviser acts as a buffer between the two parties, allowing each to negotiate tough deals, yet avoiding direct confrontation. When discussions reach an impasse, an adviser can often suggest alternative solutions to keep the dialogue going. The presence of a third party in negotiations can prompt candour and lessen tensions between you and the buyer. In addition, an adviser can cast your company in the best light to a potential acquirer, in a way that might appear improper or egotistical for an owner to do himself.

The sale of a business is a very time-consuming process. An adviser's role is to relieve you of most of the burdens and pressures associated with the sale of your business. You need to stay active and informed of the selling process, because, in the end, you will make all of the decisions. However, if an adviser has properly fulfilled his role, your involvement in the details of the sale should be minimal.

Although each situation is unique, an adviser generally handles the following functions:

- determines the advisability of a sale and potential value ranges;
- develops an appropriate selling strategy, including preparing a listing of potential domestic and foreign buyers;
- prepares an information memorandum, describing in full detail your company's operations and prospects;
- contacts potential acquirers, with a discreet and selective approach;
- schedules and conducts meetings with suitors;
- maintains dialogue with potential acquirers, providing necessary information and market data;
- negotiates the price and other terms;

- works the transaction through until completion, including helping to prepare the sale contract.

While a competent, professional adviser can add great value to the sale process, an ill-informed, inexperienced adviser can cause more harm than good. After a while, the market will come to associate your company with your adviser, and essentially view them as one entity. If your adviser has a poor reputation or no experience in disposals, it reflects poorly on you. Of course, the ultimate harm from an incompetent adviser will be the poor advice he might give. Thus, you should look for the following characteristics in choosing a professional to represent you and your company.

Professionalism

An adviser's reputation can have a profound impact on how your company is viewed by the market. Certain merger advisers have such a poor reputation that many buyers simply refuse to work with them, regardless of the merits of their clients. Be certain that your adviser has the background and credentials to do the job for you.

Experience

Nothing succeeds like success, and you certainly do not want someone 'cutting his teeth' on the sale of your company. Check to make certain that an adviser has a history of successfully initiating and completing deals involving companies of a similar size and nature as yours. Active advisers are more respected in the market; they tend to generate more interest in their clients. Go with a proven winner.

Focused effort

The sale of your business is important to you; you want it to be important to your adviser. Make certain that the adviser you choose will give your project the proper amount of attention and effort. Try to avoid advisers that take a 'listings' approach: working on dozens of companies concurrently in the hope that one will sell. While the 'numbers game' may work for them, you need a hard-working adviser dedicated to seeing your project through to a successful transaction. Good deals do not just happen; they require hard work and persistence on the part of your adviser. Find an adviser who shares this credo.

Senior level attention

Check to find out who will be working on your project within the advisory firm. Many investment banks pass on smaller deals to junior associates; large 'listings' firms employ dozens of account executives, many of whom were selling insurance in a prior career. They may have little or no experience in selling companies. The sale of your business is important to you. Find an advisory firm that is anxious enough about working on your sale to devote a senior-level partner to oversee your project. Lastly, make certain that the team that sells you its services is the same team that will deliver those services to you. Too often we have heard of instances where the 'A' team does the initial presentations, while the 'C' team does the work.

Sensitivity to your objectives

Just as no two private company owners are alike, no two owners' objectives are alike. The adviser you choose to represent your interests must be willing to take the time to completely understand your personal, financial and corporate goals. The adviser should then be willing to tailor his approach to meet those objectives. There is no such thing as a standardised marketing effort; do not even consider those advisers who refuse to conform to your wishes.

Representing only sellers

Many investment banks handle a wide variety of corporate finance activities, including trading and underwriting share and bond issues. In the same vein, many corporate finance advisers work both sides of the street: they offer merger advisory services to both buyers and sellers. This situation can cause significant conflicts of interests, especially for the seller of a private company. Buyers are constantly in the market for deals, which can represent multiple fees for a merger adviser. As a seller, you will only ever represent one fee. Conflicting loyalties cannot make an adviser a true advocate of the seller.

The best way to avoid this conflict of interest is to work with an adviser who mainly represents sellers in the market. If that is not possible, at least discuss the possible conflicts with your prospective adviser to determine how he plans to deal with the issue.

Personal compatibility

Because the selling process includes work that is alternately tedious and tense, it is important that you get along well with your adviser. You are going to depend on your adviser greatly. You should be certain from the outset that the 'chemistry' is right, and that there are no personality clashes.

Selecting an adviser

Businesses do not sell themselves; the best buyers rarely find you without an active marketing effort. For that reason, the adviser you employ has to be both experienced and aggressive. To be certain that you choose the best adviser consistent with your goals, interview several potential advisers and check their references carefully. Corporate finance firms vary greatly in size and scope – from 'one-man shops' to large investment banks. Make certain that the firm you choose has all of the capabilities you require, while being focused enough to give you top-level attention and service.

You should be very selective in choosing your merger adviser, just as you would in hiring a lawyer or accountant. The Institute of Directors, local chambers of commerce and industry associations have directories of active advisers; however, such listings should only serve as a start to your search. Seek suggestions and recommendations from friends, business associates and competitors who have sold their businesses. Personal recommendations are obviously the most reliable source of leads. By discreetly asking around and doing some homework, you should be able to develop a shortlist of competent, active advisers.

Once you have narrowed the universe down to a select few, you should take the time to individually interview each candidate, weighing the relative strengths and weaknesses of each one. Experienced corporate finance advisers should understand your desire to engage in such a 'beauty parade'; do not even consider those that will not participate in such a selection process.

As an integral part of your interviewing process, you should ask all candidates to provide references of recent clients whose businesses they have sold. Call these references and ask detailed questions about the process and their experience with that adviser. Completed deals are an adviser's only tangible evidence of success; it benefits you to take the effort to vet the record of your prospective adviser and partner in this journey.

Lastly, you should be aware of situations where an adviser representing a potential buyer approaches you on his client's behalf. At first, this situation might appear ideal: you can sell your company without going through the difficult process of marketing it, while saving yourself a fee to an adviser. It is important to remember, however, that the intermediary approaching you is looking out for his client's interests, not yours, and therefore cannot be counted on to provide proper or even reliable advice. Also, while this situation may well bypass the effort of marketing your company and an adviser's fee, it could well cost you dearly in the long run. You wind up negotiating with only one party (perhaps not even a very strong one), without the benefit of any professional advice or competing offers.

Terms and fees

Most advisers work on mainly contingent fees; they are paid a small initial fee or retainer, but by far the bulk of their fee is paid by way of a pre-arranged percentage of the total purchase price when the deal is completed. These arrangements are typically best for the seller: the main fee is paid only if the adviser is successful in selling the company. This arrangement tends to align an adviser's interests with those of his client: both have an interest in selling the company at the highest possible price.

Fees are generally based on a sliding scale of between 2 and 5 per cent on transactions in the range from £2 million to £45 million. The initial fee (or retainer), likely to be between £10,000 and £30,000, should only be payable after the adviser has produced the information memorandum.

This fee will go some way towards covering the cost of preparation. All other fees should be dependent on success. The initial fee may or may not be deducted from the eventual contingent fee (depending on the deal struck). In any event, it should be modest in size and no adviser should make money on a retainer – his profit should come only by successfully selling his client's company.

The adviser should want you to enter into a written agreement with him (called a letter of engagement). These engagement agreements can be quite long and complicated, but should explain the work the adviser will carry out and what happens if the company is not sold for whatever reason, including if you change your mind. The letter should state on what basis the fees are payable. Go through the letter with the adviser and make sure you understand it before committing to it.

It is usual that the agreement is for a period of about 12 months, after which time if the company is not sold, you review the situation.

An 'exclusive agreement' provides the adviser with the exclusive right to offer a company for sale; the adviser will receive a fee if any transaction occurs during the term of the agreement, whether the adviser introduced the buyer or not. A 'non-exclusive agreement' requires the seller to pay the adviser a fee only if the adviser introduces the party that makes the acquisition.

The most successful advisers generally only work on an exclusive basis. Those that will work on a non-exclusive basis will still devote more time and effort to those clients who have given them an exclusive sale mandate. It is important to remember that advisers have a business to run and must allocate their limited time to various clients. They will clearly put greater efforts behind those clients that have made the commitment to work exclusively with them.

It is much more difficult to maintain confidentiality and control of a sale process if you do not have one single adviser coordinating and implementing the process. In the end, it is probably best to choose the adviser with whom you are most comfortable and give them a fair shot at selling the business through an exclusive agreement.

Because the selling process is a collaborative effort, you can help to achieve a swift sale by working closely with your adviser and being totally candid about your business, its problems and its prospects. You should never circumvent your adviser by concealing possible prospects or dealing directly with those prospects yourself. This only serves to undermine your adviser's efforts, and can prove to be very counterproductive. Once you have engaged an adviser, assume the fee is a given and work closely with your adviser to achieve the best possible deal.

6 *The sale process*

Selling your business is not unlike the sale of any other product. You need to understand your product, convey its attractiveness to others, get to know the needs and wants of your prospective buyer, and sell, sell, sell.

The basic principles remain the same as in any selling situation. There are no shortcuts, and rewards usually go to those willing to put in the effort. Most importantly, you can only succeed if you constantly pay attention to your customer (in this case, the potential buyer of your company).

The owner who recognises the need for adequate preparation and effort in selling his business will go a long way towards ensuring the ultimate sale of his company at an attractive price. On the other hand, the owner who approaches the sale in an aloof or indifferent manner will tend to find that he will not attract any buyers for his company, regardless of price.

A commitment of considerable time and effort on your part is required both to maximise the value for your business and to find the 'right' buyer. The sale of your business is as important an economic decision as any you will face. It should command at least the same allocation of your time and resources as any other major project. If you are unwilling to commit these resources, if the goal does not seem worth the effort, then you should seriously reconsider selling your business.

The first step in selling your business is to make the commitment to sell. Most sophisticated buyers only want to expend efforts on opportunities where they sense a sincere interest in selling. There are enough attractive opportunities in the market that good buyers generally do not need to waste their time chasing 'tyre kickers' or sellers who are not really serious.

There are literally thousands of private businesses today that are perpetually 'for sale'. Many owners take the stance that 'anything is for sale at the right price'. These owners are continually willing to entertain all suitors that approach them. Yet, without any true desire to sell their company, these owners go about the process in a haphazard, disinterested manner and generally find their efforts unrewarded. After a while, these companies tend to be tagged as 'shop soiled' or as 'used goods'.

Nothing is as attractive the second time around. Many of the best suitors refuse to even consider companies that are perpetually 'for sale', on the market for all-comers. Most buyers assume that these companies must have some unattractive feature which prevented their sale to earlier suitors. After a while, owners of these businesses have essentially spoiled the market for their company. When the time comes that they really want or need to sell, they will probably find that the only interested parties are 'opportunistic' buyers, those who will only buy at distressed prices.

An extreme example of this occurred a few years ago to an owner of a company that manufactured lighting fixtures. On the off-chance that a buyer might pay an outrageous amount for his business, this owner was open to discussing the sale of his business with anyone who approached him. Eventually, word leaked throughout his industry that he was for sale, but only at an unrealistic price. A number of his competitors approached him about buying his company, only to be turned off by his unprofessional presentation and unrealistic expectations. Most, however, never went near, believing that the deal had become 'shop soiled'.

Three years after we first met this owner, he was told that he had developed cancer. At this point, he became desperate to sell. Yet, though we were retained to do an exhaustive search for a buyer, we could find no takers. We eventually had to cobble together a very unsatisfactory sale to his employees, which left the company burdened with debt and the owner with most of his proceeds in vendor's loan notes. The company was basically healthy and had a bright future; the main impediment to a successful sale was the stigma of being 'over-shopped'.

In our experience, few businesses actually sell because of chance meetings or direct approaches made by buyers. The best deals generally do not chase after you. Rather, you have to be aggressive in seeking them out. A proper sale of a business requires a tremendous amount of effort: preparing presentation materials, generating a universe of qualified buyers, making approaches, coordinating visits and negotiating and structuring deals. Most attempts to circumvent this effort only lead to dashed expectations or poor deals.

You are only going to sell your business once; it certainly makes sense that you do it right the first time.

Once you have decided to commit yourself to the long, arduous process of selling your business, there is a well-defined set of steps you can take to improve your chances of arranging a successful sale of your company.

1. Establish your goals and strategies

To properly address a sale of your business, you need to first establish a detailed, prioritised list of goals you want to achieve. By going through this introspective exercise, you may be surprised to find what goals are truly important to you, both personally and in terms of your company. It is clearly better to have confronted and thought through the many issues and questions involved in a sale before approaching potential buyers. Not only will this allow you to respond better to a buyer's demands, but it will impact the strategy you employ in seeking out potential buyers in the first place.

Issues that every potential seller should address range from the very broad to the very detailed, and probably should at least include the following:

- What are your main reasons for considering a sale? What do you want personally from a sale? What do you want for your company?
- What characteristics are you looking for in an acquirer?
- Do you want to remain with your company after a sale? Only for a transitional period or indefinitely to oversee growth?
- What deal structure helps you to achieve your financial goals? An all-cash deal? Do you need guaranteed loan notes? Are you willing to accept deferred terms or an earn-out in exchange for a higher price?
- Do you have children in the business and what continued role do you see for them?
- Do you want to retain the land and property separately or sell them with the business?

- Do you feel any financial or other obligations to your management team? Employees?
- Would it matter if an acquirer moved your business or merged your business into theirs?
- How important is confidentiality to you? How vital is it that your employees and customers not know that you are for sale?

Some owners want to maximise the value they receive for their company, regardless of who the buyers are. Others are unwilling to consider foreign acquirers, even if it means forgoing a higher price for their company. Some owners want to retain the autonomous integrity of their company; others do not care if their business is moved or employees are fired.

You should seek advice from others to help you think through these various issues, especially from your family, financial advisers and business associates. You should also seek out those business owners who have already sold their companies, both to get a better understanding of how they handled the process and also to learn from their experiences and mistakes. Only by going through such self-examination and general fact gathering can you determine what you really want from a sale.

Having sorted out your goals, you next need to develop a strategy to achieve them. Our experience shows that few successful deals result from a haphazard approach to selling. You need to address the sale of your company with a coordinated plan from the outset.

A well-conceived strategy will force you to define the types of acquirers you want to approach, the method of sale you want to employ, and the timetable you want to set to accomplish the sale.

If one of your main goals is to keep your management team in place and reward them for their efforts in building your company, you might want to consider first offering the company to them in a management buyout. Management buyouts often require some vendor financing and rarely offer owners the best economic deal, but they are a preferred way for many company owners to reward faithful employees.

Alternatively, if your prime goal is to cash in at the highest possible price, then you should probably pursue a strategy of approaching a broad base of potential buyers to let the 'market' determine the highest bidder.

You need to establish an anticipated schedule at the outset, and continually monitor your progress against this timetable. A typical sale, if properly employed, should take from six to nine months to complete. Table 6.2 at the end of this chapter outlines a typical timetable and chronology of the sales process.

As with any forward planning, you need to be flexible and reasonable in your plans and expectations. Markets are constantly changing; so too might your company's operating performance or future prospects. You must be nimble enough to change your plans with changing conditions. By taking a planned but flexible approach to selling your company, you will go a long way towards assuring a successful deal.

2. Prepare presentation materials

Many owners honestly believe that by simply announcing to the marketplace that their business is for sale, they can sit back and wait for the generous offers to come cascading in. Nothing could be further from the truth. The most active buyers are constantly deluged with acquisition proposals. Beset with so many opportunities, many buyers choose to pursue only those situations that are clearly and succinctly presented to them. Because it is difficult enough to get a deal done in the best of circumstances, most buyers will shy away from any situation where they are not provided with a complete and understandable description of the business at the outset.

Your company will be one of dozens of similar companies for sale at any given time; you need to make your company stand out from the crowd, to differentiate your company from all the other, mundane opportunities out there. You also need to provide potential acquirers with the relevant data they need to make a rational, informed decision on whether or not to pursue the acquisition of your company. For these reasons, it is important that you and your advisers prepare a complete descriptive information memorandum on your company before going to market. Not only will such a memorandum provide a detailed understanding of your business, it will also indicate a sincere and professional approach to selling your company.

One of an adviser's most important roles is preparing a professional information memorandum on your company, presenting your company in its best light and highlighting those points he knows will impress buyers.

If there are problems or weaknesses (as there are with most companies), the information memorandum will provide you with a forum to address them from your point of view. A descriptive information memorandum also allows you an opportunity to explain and highlight certain features of your financial statements, including a restating of both your income statements and your balance sheet.

Presenting an information memorandum on your company makes it easy for a prospective buyer to move to the next stage; he has enough of the facts at the outset to make an informed decision on whether or not to pursue your company.

A sample table of contents from an information memorandum is provided in Table 6.1. The idea is to clearly and succinctly describe your business, both its current operations and its future prospects.

It is vital that you provide a detailed analysis of your company, including a listing of your largest customers and suppliers (by volume), your employees (by salary package and length of service) and your facilities. Any acquirer will demand this information before bidding on your company; it makes sense to provide it to them at the outset. (If you are sensitive to disclosing names of customers, suppliers or employees, it is reasonable and acceptable to code these names in the memorandum, providing specifics at a later date once serious interest has been expressed by suitors.)

Some owners actually go to the opposite extreme, providing in excruciating detail all possible data on their operations. Given the short attention span of most people, we believe that this is as big a mistake as not having a sales document on your company at all.

The objective of an information memorandum is not to overwhelm a suitor, but rather to make it easy to find the relevant data on your company. You want the memorandum to be thorough, but it should also be streamlined, no more than 20–35 pages of text. The memorandum should be written so that it can be read in 15–20 minutes.

Be certain that the data you include in the information memorandum is true, accurate and complete. Various potential buyers will make decisions and, ultimately, offers based on the information provided in the memorandum. To the extent that any of it is misleading, inaccurate or incomplete, it will undermine your credibility, and could eventually jeopardise any deal that you had negotiated. We always advise clients that it is best to

Table 6.1 Sample table of contents for an information memorandum

CONTENTS

		Page
1	Introduction	1
2	Executive summary	3
	Opportunity	
	Background	
	Key products/services	
	Key financials	
	Major strengths	
	Reasons for sale	
3	History and ownership	8
4	Market analysis	10
5	Products and services	14
6	Sales and marketing	17
7	Competitive analysis	20
8	Operations and premises	24
9	Management and employees	29
10	Information systems	32
11	Financial information	33
12	Conditions under which this document is supplied	37

APPENDICES

I	Location, site plans, photographs
II	Corporate and product brochures
III	Recent press articles
IV	Financial statements and adjustments
V	Major items of equipment

make full disclosure at the outset. Any potential buyer will eventually unearth all of the facts: better to gain their trust by disclosing everything at the beginning.

In the end, having a complete information memorandum on your company will aid you in screening potential acquirers and also enable you to conserve your time. After all, if a suitor wants to meet you after reviewing the material, you know that he is attracted enough by the basics of your business to warrant going to the next step. Conversely, those parties no longer interested in your business after reviewing the memorandum will not waste your time with introductory meetings.

3. Identify prospective buyers

Over the years, most owners have probably given some thought to an informal list of prospective buyers of their companies. This list generally includes competitors, suppliers and customers. At times it may also include contacts made either socially or through various trade functions.

You may believe that one of your competitors would be the logical acquirer of your business; after all, a competitor should be able to justify a higher price by simply eliminating duplication of overheads. At times, that occurs. Yet, more often than not, your competitors are not the logical acquirers of your business.

Competitors often believe that they can expand their market share at a cost greatly below that of buying your company. In addition, competitors already know all of the problems and difficulties of your industry, and that often clouds their optimism. Consequently, competitors often end up being low bidders for your business. On top of that, by engaging in discussions with competitors, you allow them open access to your operations, employees and strategies. This can be a real detriment if a deal does not go through with them.

We have found that those who are most willing to 'pay up' for companies are those who are presently outside your field (or, at best, peripherally involved in it) but have become convinced that your industry is one in which they want to expand. These buyers are often willing to pay a premium as a cost of entry into a new area. Your company can offer an immediate presence in a new market. The costs and risks of buying an established business are significantly less than the costs and risks of starting from scratch in a new field.

Thus, you should expand your search beyond the obvious. The financial markets today are global in nature, and you should broaden your range of potential buyers to include as many different parties from as many different perspectives as possible.

Because of their presence in the marketplace, competent advisers will have a good understanding of active buyers and their acquisition criteria. Your financial advisers should be able to glean from a large universe of potential acquirers a list appropriate for you, including foreign multinational companies, large and small domestic companies, private investor groups and owner-managers who are looking for businesses to buy and run.

The ultimate list of appropriate potential candidates will depend greatly on your company and your goals. Large, synergistic corporations obviously offer you and your company different alternatives than private investor groups. You need to work closely with your advisers to generate a group of potential buyers that appear to best fit your needs and desires. Obviously, your advisers should screen all potential suitors to make certain that their interests coincide with yours, and that they have the financial wherewithal to complete a deal.

Even if you do decide to include your competitors in your search, you should approach those potential buyers outside your industry first, before engaging in any conversations with competitors. Those outside your industry will need more time to understand and get comfortable with your business. By approaching them first, you give them a head start in their preliminary groundwork. In addition, in dealing with suitors that are outside your industry, you are better able to control confidentiality. You want to minimise your exposure to leaks; those outside your industry will probably treat these matters with more discretion than those in your own field of business.

Only after you garner interest and offers from unrelated parties should you ever consider going to your competitors. With offers already in your pocket, you have tremendous leverage in getting competitors to move quickly and to act decisively. You force your competitors to make a quick decision on buying your business, lest you sell to one of the unrelated parties. This approach allows competitors minimal time to make use of confidential information or cause leaks in the market. It will also give you the upper hand in negotiating an advantageous deal from them.

4. Create a market

There are a number of different methods you can employ to sell your business, from approaching each potential acquirer separately to orchestrating an open auction. Each method has its own strengths and weaknesses.

In our experience, the best way to sell is to create a market for your business. By creating a market, you allow the competitive nature of the market to play one bidder against another to generate the highest possible price. A competitive market also presents you with an array of prospective acquirers, allowing you to weigh the relative strengths and weaknesses of each suitor.

By talking to only one party at a time, you put yourself at a competitive disadvantage. A solitary suitor will clearly know that he is the only one examining your company, and will consequently feel less compelled to offer a good deal on acceptable terms. You have little leverage in negotiating with a solitary buyer – you either accept their proposal or walk away from the deal. Additionally, even if a lone party offered you a tremendous deal, it is difficult to gauge the relative value of the offer in a vacuum, without other competing bids. In a market environment, you gain all of the leverage. Potential buyers have to step up with attractive offers at the outset, lest they lose the deal to more aggressive suitors.

The clearest way to openly market your company is through the auction process. This generally involves contacting and circulating as many information memoranda to as many suitors as possible, with bids due by a prescribed date. Those whose initial bids are deemed acceptable are allowed to visit the management at the company facilities prior to making a final, binding offer.

The upside to this process is that it gives your company the widest possible exposure, often generates the highest prices, and quickly, efficiently gets the job done. The potential problems with an auction, however, are many:

- When circulating so many memoranda (sometimes up to 500), confidentiality is almost impossible to maintain. In fact, to get as many potential buyers to participate as possible, auctions are often announced publicly.

- With confidential operating and strategic data released to so many parties, competitors will almost always walk away from an auction having gained significant new information on the selling company.
- The entire process is demoralising and disruptive to management and employees.
- Many of the more sophisticated buyers refuse to participate in openly competitive 'bid' situations. Ironically, an auction often frightens away the very buyers you want to attract.

The gravest problem with an auction is that once you start down the path, it is extremely difficult to change direction. The pressures are tremendous to accept whatever the highest offer is, whether attractive or not. After all, you have shown your hand to your competition. Your suppliers and customers are all expecting a change in ownership. And if the sale process is terminated, your management and employees will never completely trust you again. They will continually wonder when you are next going to put the company up for sale.

A middle ground does exist between talking to one party and auctioning your company: the controlled sale. Essentially, a controlled sale attempts to blend the control and confidentiality of dealing with a single suitor with the market mechanisms of an auction. With a controlled sale, the idea is to have four to six parties concurrently examining and bidding for your business. To cull the four to six interested suitors may take 50 approaches, but that still causes less exposure and distraction than approaching 500. A skilled adviser should be quite capable of generating a universe of 50 highly likely suitors.

Through a controlled sale, confidentiality and discretion are maintained, and yet you still benefit from a market environment. You can still play one bidder off against another. And if you properly choose your suitors and orchestrate the process correctly, you will be able to generate values which should approximate those on an 'open' market.

There are two important points you should remember in creating a market for your company:

(a) *Use a third party to make the initial approaches.* There is nothing discreet about you approaching someone to buy your company. Regardless of what you say or how you say it, you are approaching him with hat in hand. It is always better to have a third party, preferably a skilled professional, make the approaches for you. By making 'blind' approaches, initially seeking out a prospective buyer's appetite for acquisitions, a third party is able to maintain your confidentiality until interest is expressed. Also, a third party acts as a buffer between you and the potential acquirers, allowing you to maintain some degree of autonomy and leverage. Lastly, the process of making approaches and interfacing with an array of suitors can become very time-consuming. Your efforts are better spent profitably running your business.

(b) *Make use of confidentiality agreements.* Confidentiality agreements (or non-disclosure agreements) are essentially agreements by a prospective buyer to not disclose either: 1) that your company is for sale, or 2) any of the data on your company that will be provided. We always insist that any potential acquirer executes a confidentiality agreement before the name of our client or any other information is divulged. (Copies of two sample confidentiality agreements are given in Appendix I.)

You should be aware that confidentiality agreements are difficult to enforce. The onus is on you, the seller, to prove a breach of the agreement, and then to prove damages. It is generally very difficult to trace the exact source of any leak, let alone to prove damages. However, a confidentiality agreement does achieve a more limited goal: it sends a clear signal to any potential suitor that you consider the information you are providing to be confidential, and that you expect it to be treated as such. Generally, those who are experienced in mergers and acquisitions respect the confidential nature of any data provided to them. Confidentiality problems generally come from smaller, less-sophisticated groups with little experience in mergers and acquisitions.

5. Sell, sell, sell

The key to getting a suitor interested in your business is to get them excited about its prospects. Interest and value are often based on perception. Psychologists have shown that first impressions often determine one's ultimate perception of a situation. Fortunately, you can have a great deal of influence over how your company is perceived.

After a potential buyer expresses an interest in your business, he will undoubtedly want to arrange a visit to meet you face to face and to examine your facilities. Use this first visit as an opportunity to further excite the suitor about your business.

There are a number of things you can do to make certain that your buyer meetings are successful, including:

- Research the potential acquirer and their current operations before the meeting, so you appear informed and interested in them.
- Understand the suitor's acquisition criteria, so you can tell them why your operation could fit well with theirs.
- Set an agenda with the potential acquirer prior to the meeting, so that you are properly prepared to cover all of the issues that are important to them.
- Learn from your adviser what concerns, if any, the potential acquirer has expressed about your business, so that you can address them at the meeting.
- Be open and honest. Most acquirers have been through the process more than once and can sense when they are not getting the full story. Stubbornness at providing key company data generally signals to buyers that you are hiding something. You need to establish credibility at the outset. All businesses have problems or weaknesses; be prepared to discuss yours fairly and openly.
- Do not be suspicious. Potential acquirers may ask you a tremendous number of questions, from the significant to the obscure. Have patience and answer them as fully and honestly as possible. You would probably ask the same questions and want to get the same amount of detail if you were about to pay a lot of money for a business.

We once had a client who insisted that no potential buyer was more important than the actual running of his business. Consequently, he insisted on taking phone calls in the middle of buyer meetings and ducking out of factory tours to work at his desk. He was generally unprepared for most meetings, citing his backlog of work. Our client's skewed sense of priorities only harmed himself in the long term. Though the owner had built a fine second-tier of management capable of running his company, potential buyers got the mistaken impression that the business was too dependent on our client to ever be passed on to a new owner. Consequently, our client lost the interest of most likely suitors.

One of the major concerns of any prospective buyer is that you are selling because of some imminent problem with your business, like massive customer defections or product obsolescence. You need to be sympathetic to this concern and go to great lengths to make the buyer feel comfortable with the long-term prospects of your business.

In the end, it is imperative that you present your company in the best light to make it attractive to others. Any selling you do should be subtle, but you need to sell none the less. There is no product, nor any company, that truly sells itself.

Keep the business going

While you are going through the sale process, there are two matters on the home front that you need to address: your employees and your business.

With regard to your employees, we generally suggest informing only those employees who need to know of your plans. By announcing your plans to sell before a deal is at hand, you will create tremendous insecurity and disruption among your workforce, not to mention your customers and suppliers.

Once a deal is announced, the employees will know all about the acquirer, which will go a long way in making them more secure and comfortable about their futures. It is in the period between the decision to sell and the announcement of a deal, when the future is so uncertain, that employees are so concerned about their own security.

If a sale is conducted properly, you should be able to go through most of the process without employees ever finding out. Conduct factory tours under a guise, and have meetings and phone conversations off-site. The only way that your employees will have suspicions is if you start to act suspiciously.

With regard to your business, you need to continue to operate for the long term, as if no sale were going to occur. The most obvious reason for this is that the sale process may fail. Given the possibility that you

Table 6.2 Typical timetable/chronology of the sales process

Month 1
- Select adviser; work together in collating necessary information
- Hold tax planning meeting
- Start pre-sale grooming as appropriate
- Adviser prepares information memorandum
- Adviser starts researching possible acquirers approach list
- Discuss and approve list and strategy with adviser

Months 2–3
- Adviser makes approaches
- Discuss and screen responses with adviser
- Adviser obtains confidentiality agreement from interested parties
- Adviser supplies information memorandum

Months 3–4
- Assess initial levels of interest
- Adviser arranges initial meetings off-site
- Adviser continues to expand approach list and make new approaches
- Adviser arranges site visits for truly interested parties

Months 4–5
- Adviser generates initial offers
- Sort offers and decide which to pursue
- Adviser arranges follow-up site visits and provides additional information
- Adviser negotiates between various top few suitors to elicit highest offers
- Evaluate offers with adviser
- Decide on a deal
- Negotiate and sign up heads of agreement with preferred purchaser

Months 5–6
- Lawyer aided by adviser negotiates sale and purchase contract
- Buyer starts due diligence

Months 7–8
- Lawyers finally agree sale and purchase agreement and disclosures
- Buyer (and his financiers) completes all due diligence
- Sign contract
- Complete deal and receive consideration

---

may continue to own your company, it obviously makes sense for you to keep it running as well as possible.

Too many owners take their eyes off the running of their company in anticipation of a sale. This is a grave mistake. You need to keep your business operating at peak performance throughout the process to demonstrate its worth to suitors. Nothing can impair your chances of maximising value more than showing disappointing operating results in the middle of negotiations. Remember, interest and value are often based primarily on perception. If your profits or prospects drop, so too will your company's value and your negotiating strength.

There is a temptation for owners to sacrifice the future for the present. In an effort to show attractive earnings, many owners curtail necessary spending on such things as advertising and development, and raise prices to show immediate margin increases. Yet, such short-term thinking will probably backfire on you. First, if you do not sell your business, you will have to live with the long-term consequences of such moves. Secondly, you should always assume that buyers are at least as canny as you are; they will probably eventually uncover any such financial manoeuvring. When they do, you will lose credibility, and may also lose a deal.

7 *Negotiating and structuring the optimal deal*

In the process of building your company, you have undoubtedly spent time at the negotiating table, arranging everything from lease renewals to wage rounds. Yet, in terms of magnitude, time and effort, there is probably very little that will prepare you for the process of negotiating, structuring and closing the sale of your business.

The sale of your business is an all-encompassing matter. Virtually every part of your company will be under scrutiny and will somehow enter into the deal – including the state of your premises, your management, employees, tax liabilities, pension schemes and outstanding litigation.

Too many owners have consummate faith in their negotiating skills. They enter into negotiations totally unprepared for the enormous task ahead. These owners tend to focus solely on the price they get for their company, leaving the rest of the details to their advisers to work out. Unfortunately, this attitude can lead to very costly mistakes.

Prior to entering into any negotiation to sell your business, you need to define clear and obtainable goals, and then determine a coherent strategy to achieve those goals. You also need to prepare specific information and arguments to quantitatively and analytically support your positions and objectives.

Negotiations are a process of give and take. It is vital that you predetermine what trade-offs you are willing to accept to attain your primary goals.

The two parties to any negotiation generally approach a pending transaction from different perspectives – with completely different, sometimes conflicting, motivations. You, the seller, are looking for the highest price with the fewest possible contingencies. The prospective buyer is seeking the lowest price with the most favourable terms. Depending on your relative bargaining power, one party may have more negotiating leverage than the other – one side may want or need the deal more.

Nevertheless, negotiations tend to lead to successful deals only when both sides approach the talks with an eye towards compromise. Each party needs to believe that he achieved most of his goals, or no deal will ever be consummated. Consequently, each side needs to be willing to accommodate the other.

We generally suggest to our clients that they enter negotiations with an attitude of creating mutually beneficial solutions to impasses or road-blocks. Successfully negotiated deals involve strategic trade-offs. By being flexible and creative, working with your opponent to seek joint solutions to problems, you will probably be able to mould a deal acceptable to both parties.

The right 'chemistry' between a buyer and seller can go a long way towards cementing a deal. You will dramatically increase the probability of a successful deal by working collaboratively with a prospective buyer.

While every negotiation involves unique circumstances, there are a number of universal tips that apply to most situations. Here are 10 practical tips for successful negotiations.

1. *Keep your eyes on your goals.* Prioritise your objectives up front. Do not get bogged down on unimportant or non-essential issues. Minor points can be addressed after the major issues are resolved. Focus primarily on those goals that are important to you.
2. *Do not expect to win every battle.* You will probably never negotiate a deal if you insist on winning every argument. Negotiations require compromise; you need to let the other side win a few points to get anywhere in negotiations. Indeed, by conceding on some points, you can trade-off to win issues really essential to you. The best deals are so-called 'win-win' situations, where both sides end up getting most of what they want. Just focus on winning those points that are important to you.

3. *Understand the other side's wants and needs.* It is often helpful to put yourself in your opponent's shoes, to understand their reasons for buying your company. Once you see the deal from their vantage point, you will be better able to present your goals in a manner acceptable to them.

   If you can determine what is important to the other side and can figure out a way to give them what they want, they should be willing to accommodate you on your points. An example: many buyers are unwilling to take substantial goodwill on to their balance sheets, thus limiting the amount they are willing to pay over your company's stated net worth. Solution: take some of the value by way of an on-going consultancy agreement. This might not be the most tax-effective solution, but it allows the buyer to achieve his goal of minimising goodwill, while still providing you with the price you seek.

4. *Do not get emotional.* Do not get caught up in the drama of the event, or take matters personally. If you cannot trust yourself to remain calm at negotiations, stay away and let your advisers handle these matters for you.

   You may be surprised how much you can obtain from buyers if you do not reveal your thoughts through your emotions. A client of ours was once hopeful of getting £17 million for his distribution business. He was overjoyed when a prospective buyer threw out an offer of £20 million at the initial negotiating meeting. By maintaining his composure and controlling his emotions, our client was ultimately able to negotiate the buyer up to £22 million.

   Of course, the antithesis occurs as well. Do not be upset or put off by low initial offers. A buyer is only doing his job by trying to buy your company for as little as possible. Do not let your ego either be easily bruised or get in the way of selling your business. Keep calm and stay the course. Negotiations are a process; they take time, patience and a tremendous amount of bargaining.

5. *Be flexible.* The idea of negotiations is to achieve most of your goals through compromise. Always be willing to think of or listen to alternative proposals. As long as you achieve your primary goals, be flexible as to how you get there. There are ways around most log-jams; be creative and work collectively with your opponent to find solutions that work for both parties.

6. *Listen.* Let your opponent do most of the talking. By listening, you draw your opponent out and encourage him to disclose his bargaining position or his ultimate goals. The 'winner' of a negotiation is not the one who controls the conversation, but rather the one who walks away with what he wanted.

7. *Never be afraid to walk away from a deal.* It is important that you never emotionally commit yourself to a buyer until after a deal has been negotiated. Buyers can clearly sense if you want a deal too badly and will naturally take advantage of the situation. To maintain negotiating leverage, you must always be willing to walk away from any deal that does not satisfy your basic requirements. Never put yourself in a position where you feel pressured to take a deal; always leave yourself room to walk. And yet . . .

8. *Never threaten to walk away from a deal unless you mean it.* You only get to walk once. After that, you have lost all credibility and leverage. Walking away from negotiations should only be used as a last resort, not as one of your many negotiating tools.

9. *Deal honestly and openly.* To extract the best deal from a buyer, you must first build an atmosphere of trust. If you have been overtly sly with prospective buyers, or have not been particularly forthcoming, you force buyers to adopt a cautious attitude towards you and your company. You will never achieve a premium deal from a cautious, uncertain buyer.

    Make a policy of cooperating with all prospective buyers. By being honest and open, you will help to make the buyer more comfortable and confident, which will ultimately put him in a position to offer his most attractive deal.

    Many owners feel the need to bluff or lie to achieve their objectives. By creating fictitious offers from ghost buyers, these owners hope to get suitors to bid against themselves. We have rarely seen this ploy work; indeed, the results are generally counter-productive. When uncovered (and they usually are), these ploys will prove embarrassing at best, and could eventually undermine a deal.

10. *Do not over-negotiate.* Stop when you have achieved your goals. Learn to stop when you are ahead. You never know when a buyer is ready to call it quits; by continuing to push and prod, you may quickly find out.

Always maintain a positive negotiating environment. It is a long, arduous road to consummate a transaction; you want the buyer to be sufficiently motivated to get there. Likewise, to the extent that you remain to run the company, you will end up working closely with your former opponent. If the buyer believed that you acted callously or inappropriately in negotiating the deal, continuing relations with your new owner may be strained.

Negotiations demand considerable patience, which can cause emotional wear and tear on sellers. Recognise that it may take quite a while to finally reach the finish line, and there will be quite a number of hurdles before you get there. Little in life that is worthwhile comes quickly or easily.

Because anxiety may affect your negotiating skills, it is often advisable to have a third party do most of the negotiating for you. This shelters you from most of the daily combat; you participate only when 'broad' agreements have been reached.

Most owners are too close to their business to be rational in candidly assessing their situation. Emotions and enthusiasms get the best of all of us. By staying away from the initial stages of negotiations, you are able to maintain a buffer between you and the 'deal'. Allowing a third party to negotiate the early stages of a transaction gives you the upper hand. You get involved only when a pending deal displays sufficient momentum to warrant your participation.

One of our recent clients decided to ignore our advice and got intimately involved in negotiating the sale of his business. He wanted to actively participate in every discussion that related to his company and his deal. As a manufacturer of medical diagnostic equipment, our client's company naturally had some exposure to product liability claims. However, our client's stellar track record and long experience in the field suggested rather minimal exposure to the problem. Indeed, product liability was not initially a major concern to the potential buyer.

None the less, our client was the worrying type. He continually focused discussions on the product liability issue, repeatedly refusing to indemnify against future claims. Our client's anxiety over this point soon made the prospective buyer nervous.

After considerable examination of the matter, the buyer eventually insisted on a large three-year escrow to cover any potential product liability claims. By being too close to the problem, by not seeing the forest for the trees, our client's participation in the negotiations resulted in part of his purchase price being tied up for three years. Had our client not continually harped on the issue, the buyer would undoubtedly have taken a less stringent position on the matter.

Even when negotiating with a sincere, interested buyer, discussions can collapse if a common ground cannot be found. Indeed, you may enter into negotiations with a number of parties, most of which will result in no deal. However friendly or acrimonious the discussions, however far apart you and a buyer are, you should always conclude negotiations on a positive note. Emphasise both the points you agreed on and your continued willingness to resume talks at a later date.

It never pays to burn bridges. You never know how or when the prospective buyer could be useful to you in the future. By leaving the door ajar, you allow both sides the opportunity to re-open negotiations at a later date, should one party or both reconsider their position.

The deal

The negotiations of a deal do not begin and end with the determination of a purchase price. It is true that the central issue in most negotiations is price. However, matters such as structure, terms, tax indemnities, employment agreements, representations and warranties of the seller, and conditions and contingencies on the deal are all integral parts of any deal. These 'peripheral' matters, often overlooked by owners, can have a profound effect on the economics of any deal.

Determining the structure and terms of a transaction can be the most challenging aspect of any deal. Various structures and terms offer abundant opportunities for you to creatively mould a deal to meet your specific needs. Yet, before you enter any negotiation, you need to understand both the differing structures and terms that are available, and their potential ramifications on your deal. Below we provide an overview of the basic deal structures and terms that have evolved over time.

Deal structure

The structure of a transaction refers to the legal and financial form that the deal takes.

Certain structures may be more appropriate than others, depending on your specific cash requirements, security and diversification goals, and tax strategies. Often, a buyer's circumstances and objectives are at odds with the seller's. You need to understand how your transaction is affected by various structures, and then select the structure that most benefits you. The ultimate structure, of course, will generally be a compromise to balance your needs and wants with those of the buyer.

There are basically two ways to acquire a business:

1. A share purchase – whereby the acquirer buys all the shares for cash or other consideration.
2. A trade and asset purchase – whereby the acquirer does not buy the company but buys the business and the underlying assets, for cash or other consideration.

A share purchase essentially involves the purchase of all a company's share capital for cash, securities or other consideration. In such a transaction, a buyer purchases the company's balance sheet 'as is', indirectly buying all of the company's assets at their carried (or, in the case of fixed assets, depreciated) value and assuming all of the company's stated and unstated liabilities. The company's tax basis in the assets remains unchanged. The purchaser's cost for tax purposes is equal to the purchase price.

In a trade and asset purchase, an acquirer purchases some or all of a company's assets in exchange for cash, securities, or other property. Concurrent with the purchase, the acquirer assumes some or all of the company's stated liabilities. Typically, an asset purchase includes all of the tangible and intangible assets used in the business, including land and buildings, equipment, stock, debtors and patents, to name but a few. Once assets are sold, owners of the selling companies often liquidate their companies and distribute all of the proceeds to the shareholders. This structure can give rise to a double tax charge, once at the corporate level and once at the shareholder level.

Both a share purchase and an asset purchase contain certain inherent advantages and disadvantages for buyers and sellers alike.

From a buyer's perspective, there are two main distinctions between an asset purchase and a share purchase. In a share purchase, an acquirer maintains your company's balance sheet intact. In an asset purchase, however, an acquirer can allocate the purchase price over the various assets acquired. Buyers typically prefer asset deals, primarily because this structure allows them to 'step up' assets to their fair market value. By writing up assets to their fair market value, buyers can minimise the 'goodwill' in a deal.

'Goodwill' is an intangible that reflects the excess over the selling company's net assets that is paid to acquire a business. Goodwill is essentially 'air'; it represents the intangible premium above net worth that an acquirer is willing to pay to buy a company's business and its future earnings stream.

Buyers are often wary of paying too high a premium for a company because of the goodwill they will have to recognise. Because it is usually amortised over 20 years, goodwill can generate a long-term drag on earnings. It also tends to inflate a buyer's balance sheet with too much in the way of intangible assets. Financial analysts and institutional investors tend to penalise companies that have too much goodwill on their balance sheets.

The second major advantage of an asset deal to buyers is that the structure shields an acquirer from any unknown, undisclosed or contingent liabilities. In an asset purchase, a buyer generally assumes only those liabilities that are specifically outlined in the purchase agreement. Indeed, to protect himself, a buyer generally insists upon an express disclaimer and exclusion of all other seller liabilities. Conversely, in a share deal, a buyer assumes all of the liabilities of your company, whether disclosed or undisclosed, whether on the balance sheet or off. Horror stories abound of acquirers unknowingly buying into undisclosed or unknown litigation or tax liabilities.

Both the ability to 'step up' assets and the concern over hidden liabilities argue strongly for buyers to structure asset deals. However, mitigating factors need to be weighed by buyers: many intangible assets and leases may not be easily assignable. Leases, especially those with 'below market' terms, need to be either renegotiated or assigned in an asset deal, often at significantly increased costs.

In addition, many businesses operate under various contractual rights, such as franchises, licences, distribution agreements, or union agreements, most of which are not assignable without consent. A share purchase leaves these contracts intact, whereas an asset deal will require renegotiation, perhaps resulting in less favourable terms.

As a seller, however, you generally have a different point of view on the matter of a share purchase versus an asset purchase. Most sellers prefer a share transaction to an asset transaction, for the following reasons.

Taxes

An asset sale usually results in double taxation; the selling company pays corporation tax on the sale of the assets, and the shareholders pay personal tax when the proceeds are distributed. In contrast, a share sale results in only one tax to the sellers: a capital gains tax on the difference between the sellers' base cost and their total proceeds. Thus, the incremental tax savings in a share sale can be significant.

Cost

An asset deal is generally more complex, expensive and time-consuming than a share deal. An asset transaction requires a legal transfer of each asset, together with the novation of all contracts. In addition, it can be a long and costly endeavour to renegotiate or obtain consents to assign leases, licences or other contract rights. A share sale, on the other hand, generally requires only one contract. While that contract will contain numerous warranties and indemnities, which need to be negotiated between the parties, a share sale is certainly a simpler and cheaper transaction for sellers.

Liabilities

In an asset deal, a buyer specifically limits his assumption of liabilities to those outlined in the purchase agreement. (Note that irrespective of what is stated in the agreement, all employee terms and rights are transferred to a buyer in an asset deal.) In a share deal, the buyer directly assumes all corporate liabilities, including contingent and unknown liabilities. You should be aware that in a share deal, you will be called on to list all known company liabilities and indemnify a buyer against any undisclosed liabilities. Thus, a share deal is not as advantageous as it appears; you will generally still remain exposed for contingent or undisclosed liabilities relating to events that occurred in your company up until completion.

Deal terms

Price and terms are intimately intertwined; one is generally very dependent on the other. An integral part of the price of a deal is the terms under which the price is paid. There is an often-used phrase in the merger business: 'You name the price, and I'll name the terms.' Clearly, there is a significant difference between a deal for £25 million in cash and a deal for £25 million in a 5 per cent, 20-year unsecured loan note. Owners who focus on maximising price in such a cavalier manner without regard to terms generally wind up only fooling themselves.

Alternatively, some owners approach the sale of their company with only one acceptable term in mind: cash. A cash deal is certainly the cleanest method of payment; it also offers the least risk. However, a cash transaction may not be the most logical way to fulfil your liquidity objectives. Alternative methods would allow you to spread out, defer or possibly eliminate a taxable gain. Other terms will allow you to continue to share in the growth or profitability of your company. Lastly, you may find that by being flexible, you can get a significantly better overall deal than would be possible with an all-cash transaction. Sometimes, regardless of your preferences, the only way that you will ever get a buyer to pay your price is by being flexible on the terms.

In reality, most sales of private, middle-market companies are not all-cash deals. Most deals involve varying combinations of cash, shares, loan notes, non-compete payments, consulting/employment agreements, royalties and contingent 'earn-outs'. At times, a buyer cannot fund all of the purchase price in cash and needs you to finance part of the deal. Alternatively, a buyer may want part of the purchase price to be in the form of a tax deductible employment agreement or non-compete payment, to provide him with some tax relief.

The key to negotiating the optimal deal is to decide at the outset what price and what terms will be acceptable to you. Remember that there is generally a very tight interplay between price and terms; flexibility or rigidity in one generally affects the other. With that in mind, below is a brief elaboration of the most common terms you will encounter.

Loan notes

Buyers generally ask sellers to take loan notes either to help finance part of the purchase price, or because the buyers do not want to finance the transaction themselves in the commercial markets. Notes offer many opportunities to creatively balance buyers' and sellers' interests, especially in the areas of amortisation and security.

One way to structure a mutually acceptable note is to evaluate various amortisation options, including 'interest only' periods and 'balloon' payments, as alternatives to equal instalments of interest and principal.

There are many different types of loan notes, each type used to achieve a different end. A purchaser may ask vendors to accept an unsecured loan note. This is in effect the vendor lending the purchaser money to buy the shares. This can be risky, as the true worth of the loan note depends upon the purchaser's ability to pay the interest and capital on the due dates. If the purchaser is unable to do so, the vendor has little redress. A guaranteed loan note (often guaranteed by a bank) is a very useful way of obtaining a great amount of security on a loan and some tax planning advantages for the vendor.

Employment and consultancy agreements

There are very legitimate reasons for buyers to pay owners for continued consulting or employment: to compensate them for vital services rendered. However, payments for consulting or employment also offer fertile ground for buyers to pay you additional money for your business, while providing them with some tax relief.

By offering consultancy agreements with few obligations attached, or inflating the salary in an employment agreement, buyers are able to funnel more money to a seller, in effect increasing the purchase price. This is attractive to acquirers because employment payments are deductible, thus providing buyers with some tax benefits. All consideration that is paid for your shares or assets comes from after-tax money. Employment or consultancy payments come from pre-tax money. However the tax position of the vendor could be significantly worse, as this income will be subject to income tax. A reasonable balance needs to be struck.

Pension payments

If the vendor does not already have a fully funded pension scheme, a purchaser can make a pension contribution to a scheme set up for the vendor. This can be very effective, as corporate tax relief can be obtained for such a payment.

Payments for covenants not to compete ('non-compete payments')

It is customary for all purchase agreements to include a 'covenant not to compete' – in effect, a clause preventing owners from directly or indirectly competing with their companies once they have sold. Most buyers will insist on some form of non-compete. After all, a company's most important asset is its people. A buyer's worst nightmare is that he buys you out, only to have you go across the street to establish a competing business. A non-compete covenant ostensibly enhances the value of your business.

However, owing to the tax treatment, the value for the non-compete covenant is usually rolled into the total purchase price. It is part of the whole consideration and subject to capital gains tax for the vendor. Even if a purchaser separated the payment, the non-compete covenant would be part of his acquisition cost.

Contingent payments/earn-outs

Earn-outs are generally a way to resolve differences of opinion over the value of a company by basing part of the purchase price on the future performance of the company.

Sellers are typically very optimistic about future prospects; buyers tend to be more conservative. An earn-out is a mechanism to acknowledge the seller's optimism towards the future, but to compensate such optimism only if and when the results are realised. A seller gains some assurance that the ultimate purchase price fairly reflects the future earnings potential, while the purchaser guards against paying too much for a company.

Earn-outs tend to be based on the future operating performance of the selling company. Typical earn-outs provide for additional payments to a seller if profits exceed agreed-upon levels, or a sharing of profits over a pre-set time frame. Two differing examples: an earn-out that provides for 5 per cent of sales over a five-year period versus one that allows for 15 per cent of operating profit until £3 million is earned. The structure generally depends on the motivations and the concerns of the buyer.

Contingent earn-outs make the most sense when an owner is staying on to run his company after the sale. The owner can thus have a direct impact on his company's performance and therefore his future payments. Buyers often use earn-outs as a way to continue to provide incentives to sellers who otherwise would have no economic interest in the company they continue to operate. Earn-outs provide sellers with an opportunity to continue to participate in the growth and profitability of their company.

Payments can take many forms: they can be structured as royalties, as bonuses, or as part of the consideration paid for the business. If an earn-out is paid as part of the consideration for the business, it must be structured very carefully so that a tax liability only occurs when the earn-out is paid. If it is structured improperly, you might pay tax on monies you never receive. Obviously, most acquirers would prefer to structure contingent payments as bonuses or royalties, as these payments are deductible expenses.

While attractive in theory, earn-outs can be difficult to administer in practice. From the start, both parties need to agree on definitions of certain key terms used to calculate the contingent payment, like 'earnings', 'profits', or 'net income'. Also, to fairly determine earnings, a purchaser should agree to operate the business as a separate entity, consistent with past practice (including maintenance of accounting standards). Obviously, it is difficult to gauge the performance of an acquired company if it is combined with or merged into the buyer's operation.

Sellers should also clarify how management charges or inter-company transactions may affect their ability to reach the earn-out goals. Issues such as depreciation, non-recurring expenses and on-going capital expenditures also need to be addressed.

In the end, no legal document can fully protect both parties in an earn-out. There are an infinite number of administrative problems to work out, most of which can never be fully or properly addressed in a contract. For earn-outs to work, both buyer and seller must ultimately have an implicit, 'good faith' trust in one another.

Because of the contingent nature of earn-outs, we generally advise clients that they should be reasonably content with all of the other aspects of their deal, as if those aspects were the only consideration they will receive. Before accepting an earn-out, you should recognise that you may earn nothing from the earn-out, that forces beyond your control may deny you any future payments. Therefore, you must be satisfied with the initial 'down payment' as compensation for your company. Any earn-out payments, if and when they come, are 'gravy'.

Shares

You may be offered shares in the purchaser as part of your payment. If this is the case, there are a number of aspects that should be considered.

By accepting shares, you are in fact making an investment in your buyer. It is incumbent on you to learn as much as you can about the appropriateness and advisability of that investment. After all, your purchaser will carry out due diligence before acquiring your company. You should perform no less an examination of the buyer.

If the shares are listed on a stock market, you will be able to assess their current value. However, depending on the terms of the purchase and sale agreement, you may not be allowed to trade the shares for a period of time (typically 12 to 18 months), which is referred to as the 'lock in'. Throughout this time, the value of your shares can rise and fall, and you will be unable to sell them.

From our perspective, if you are enamoured with the prospects of the stock of your prospective acquirer, it often makes more economic sense just to use some of your cash proceeds to buy those shares in the open market.

If the purchaser's shares are not listed on a stock market, it is important to understand that you may not be able to sell them and convert them into cash. Sometimes purchasers have plans for flotation, and hold this up as an attractive scenario. You must be aware that many proposed flotations do not happen, and a minority stake in an unlisted company has little value.

Some purchasers insist that you take some of your consideration as shares in their company. The tax consequences of accepting shares can usually be mitigated by electing to do a 'share for share' exchange, whereby you roll over the base cost of your shares into the new ones, and are taxed only when they are sold. Thus, you can defer the recognition of your gain and the resultant tax until some point in the future.

Tax considerations

Taxation is at best a complicated topic. Taxation relating to the sale of a business is especially so. The comments in this book are only a general guide and description. No reader should rely on the statements made, for they are less than complete and will be out of date very quickly. Instead you should take good professional advice.

Capital gains tax

Since April 1998 when business asset taper relief was introduced, many vendors have assumed that they will be able to pay capital gains tax at an effective rate of 10 per cent of the overall gain. While in many instances this will be the case, there are a number of potential pitfalls that need early action if they are to be avoided. Beware!

The correct starting point is to look at the base cost of your shares. You may be entitled to indexation allowance on the increase in their value from March 1982 till April 1998 (when taper relief took over). Indexation for the full period from March 1982 to April 1998 effectively doubles the March 1982 value.

Taper relief reduces the gains on all types of assets, but a more generous version is available for disposals of 'business assets' than for non-business assets. For disposals from 6 April 2002, the period of taper relief operates as shown in Table 7.1.

As can be seen, there is a significant advantage in the shares qualifying as a business asset. However, while shares in an unquoted trading company would usually qualify as a business asset, the actual assets within the company can have an effect on the eligibility of the shares to be treated as business assets. For example, if the company has a property that it lets (or rents out to a third party), then that property is not a business asset. Similarly, if the company has cash on deposit, which is not needed for trading, then the surplus cash is not a business asset. The general rule is that if the non-business assets exceed 20 per cent of the value of the com-

Table 7.1 Taper relief

Gains on disposal of business assets		Gains on disposal of non-business assets	
Numer of whole years in qualifying period	Percentage of gain chargeable	Number of whole years in qualifying period	Percentage of gain chargeable
1	50	1	100
2	25	2	100
3	25	3	95
4	25	4	90
5	25	5	85
6	25	6	80
7	25	7	75
8	25	8	70
9	25	9	65
10 or more	25	10 or more	60

pany, they will taint the whole of the company so that business asset taper relief will not be available. There may be periods during which the company qualifies for the relief and other periods when it does not. Any capital gain on the sale of shares is apportioned between business asset gains and non-business asset gains on a pro-rata basis equivalent to the periods for which the company does, and does not, qualify for business asset relief.

Having outgrown their original premises, many owners acquire new facilities and let the old ones. This very understandable decision has unforeseen negative consequences, as outlined above.

Since 6 April 1998, for an individual shareholder to qualify, he must have owned at least 25 per cent of the voting shares in the company, or been an employee of the company and owned at least 5 per cent. The rules changed on 6 April 2000, so that an individual need only own shares (no matter how many) in a qualifying trading company. However, if you qualified since 6 April 2000, but did not qualify before, say because you were not an employee but owned 20 per cent, then again you have to be very careful. The amount of business asset taper relief will be time-apportioned between 6 April 1998 to 6 April 2000 and then to the date of sale, with only the latter period qualifying.

The tainting of the business assets and the time apportionment of ownership mean that planning in advance is advisable, and a little effort can generally ensure that the problems are circumvented.

A typical way is to change the ownership of the shares, two years before the sale, by way of a trust, and thus start the taper relief clock again. Similarly non-qualifying assets can be removed from the company in advance of sale, and the taper relief clock restarted. Where there is a transfer of assets between husband and wife, a no gain/no loss rule applies. When the receiving spouse disposes of the asset, taper relief is computed as if that individual had owned the shares for the period when they were actually owned by the transferring spouse. If the shares are a business asset of, say, the husband, it will be advantageous to transfer the wife's to him, so that those shares are re-characterised as his business assets.

If part of your consideration takes the form of shares or loan notes in the acquiring company, further complications arise. If the acquiring company is an unquoted trading company, then the shares in that company may also qualify for business asset taper relief. However, if the acquiring company is quoted, unless the vendor becomes an employee of the acquirer the new shares would not qualify for taper relief, and the gain would be time apportioned.

Similarly, if the acquirer issues loan notes, the form of the loan notes is very important. If the loan notes are qualifying corporate bonds (QCB), they will not be effective for taper relief and the amount of the taxable gain will be quantified at the time that you receive the loan notes. If the loan notes are non-QCBs, then they will continue to qualify for taper relief, provided that in the case of non-QCBs issued by a quoted company, the employment criterion is met.

This is a very complicated area, and specific advice is needed in each and every situation. You need advisors who deal regularly with these issues as the legislation changes frequently.

Inheritance tax

A situation that is frequently overlooked by vendors is the change in their inheritance tax position. Inheritance tax, which is charged on the value of your estate when you die, is currently 40 per cent of the value on all your estate in excess of £255,000 (April 2003). There are a number of exemptions, in particular business property relief, which for many vendors means that the shares that they own in their company are exempt. As soon as those shares are sold, a potential inheritance tax situation arises.

The proper time to commence tax planning is prior to any sale, not just for capital gains tax, but also to put all your affairs in order. While inheritance tax is never paid by the deceased, his family and beneficiaries will have to pay it!

Summary

As should be obvious in reading this chapter, there are many complex legal, accounting, regulatory and tax issues involved in negotiating and structuring a deal. Differing deal structures offer differing tax ramifications. On top of that, tax laws and accounting standards are constantly changing.

A prudent business owner will recognise the limits of his knowledge of these areas and will engage expert advisers to help guide him through the maze. The information in this book is cursory in its coverage of the important legal, accounting and tax aspects of acquisitions. It cannot serve as a substitute for professional advice.

Many business owners naturally turn to their long-time accountants and lawyers for such advice. Because of their intimate knowledge of both the selling company and the personal affairs of the owner, these professionals are often the correct choice. However, many accountants and lawyers who are perfectly capable of handling routine affairs are totally incapable of handling the many complex aspects of a sale. The area of mergers and acquisitions is considered a speciality; those professionals with specific experience in this area generally have an advantage over those who do not. Experienced professionals pay for themselves many times over, not only for what they advise you to do, but also for what they advise you not to do.

If a corporate acquirer is coming to a negotiating table with a major law or accounting firm advising him, you need to match him with equivalent experience and ability. After all, you do not want your accountant and legal adviser learning on your deal. Thus it may behove you to seek a different set of professionals to arrange the sale of your company than your customary advisers.

As a side issue, you should always be aware of the inherent conflict of interest in retaining your customary advisers. After all, your company is probably a major account to both your law and accounting firms. Naturally, these professionals will be concerned about losing your business after the deal is done.

There is a natural, unavoidable conflict that cannot help but colour the relationship between you and your professionals. By hiring outsiders, you totally eliminate this problem.

If you do decide to retain your regular professionals, you might consider offering a generous severance payment, contingent on the deal closing, in order to align their interests with yours. It is always important to keep your professionals oriented towards the deal. After all, once you have made a decision to sell, you want everyone on your team focused on your goals.

Heads of agreement

Once two parties reach an agreement in principal as to the basic price, structure and terms of a transaction, they typically enter into what is termed a 'heads of agreement' (also referred to as a 'letter of intent'.) The heads of agreement is a written outline of the general understanding between buyer and seller, serving to clarify in writing the basic terms of the deal. The heads of agreement can be viewed as a marker on the road to a completed deal; both sides stop by the side to record in writing the basic agreements that have been reached thus far in the process.

Typically drafted by the buyer, the heads of agreement generally sets out the proposed price, terms and structure of a transaction, as well as the conditions and contingencies on completing the deal.

In most instances, the heads of agreement do not create a binding obligation; rather, they spell out the 'intent' of both parties to close the transaction along the lines of the terms presented. However, heads of agreement generally do create binding obligations on each side to continue to maintain confidentiality, to grant a period of exclusivity and to bear their own legal and accounting expenses.

The period of exclusivity basically prohibits you from approaching other potential purchasers or negotiating with other parties for a specified time frame (generally 45–90 days). Most buyers will insist on an exclusivity clause, primarily to allow themselves sufficient time to complete their detailed examination of your company and to negotiate and execute a binding purchase agreement. Buyers have to expend considerable time, effort and expense in completing a deal; they naturally only want to proceed if they can get a like commitment out of you. If you are serious about a specific buyer and a specific deal, you should be willing to provide this 'exclusive' window of time.

There are two main advantages for a seller to enter into a heads of agreement:

1. It clearly and succinctly outlines the basic terms of the deal for all parties to witness. A heads of agreement provides written proof of mutually agreed terms and conditions, should either party attempt to change the deal or re-negotiate later on.
2. You obtain a moral, if not legal, commitment from a buyer to use his good faith efforts to complete on the transaction outlined in the letter. (Incidentally, you also get an indirect financial commitment, in that a heads of agreement will cost the buyer significant legal fees to draft.)

Though each heads of agreement is unique in reflecting the specific circumstances of each transaction, most cover the following issues:

- *The price and terms of the deal.* The price may be expressed as a fixed amount or as a formula (often expressed as the selling company's net worth, plus or minus a fixed amount, with the net worth to be determined as of the day of completion). There is generally a clause to cover what happens to the company's profits between the date of the heads of agreement and completion, and how those profits are to be paid out. Basic details of the consideration (whether cash, terms of any loan notes, shares, etc) should be stated clearly.

- *The structure of the deal.* This section should address whether the transaction is structured as purchase of shares or assets, and should include descriptions of special accounting or tax considerations inherent in the proposed structure.
- *The time frame for negotiating the purchase agreement.* Generally 45–90 days, during which time most acquirers demand an exclusivity clause. Most heads of agreement self-terminate at the end of the period.
- *The specifics of any employment agreements, consulting agreements or covenants not-to-compete.* Issues surrounding employment and consulting agreements include the term, salary and specific duties to be performed. Non-compete covenants need to be defined in terms of activity, time and place.
- *The conditions and contingencies of the deal.* A listing of the conditions and contingencies that must be met prior to a close, such as financing for the deal, a complete audit of your company's books, or regulatory approvals. If one of the conditions is a full examination (due diligence) of your company, the procedures and time frame under which that examination takes place should be clearly defined.

An example of a 'typical' heads of agreement is provided in Appendix II.

Because the heads of agreement may include some legally binding clauses, it is not advisable for you to enter into one without first consulting your legal adviser.

Unlike many property deals, most transactions involving companies do not include the payment of a deposit. A prospective buyer of your company makes an offer based on very cursory data, almost all of it supplied by you. Thus, in making an offer, the buyer has assumed that all of the information you have provided is accurate and complete. It is rare that buyers will pay a deposit on an offer which is based on totally unverified information.

Instead, prior to entering into a heads of agreement with a suitor, do your homework on your prospective acquirer. Convince yourself of their ability to finance the acquisition of your company. Review their history of prior acquisitions: examine both their record of completing deals and their record of success with those companies after acquisition. Diligent examination of the prospective buyer will provide a much higher degree of comfort than any deposit. After all, you are not going through this process merely to pocket a deposit; you are seeking to sell your company.

Lastly, you should not equate the execution of a heads of agreement with the completion of a deal. A heads of agreement is but one step, albeit an important one, on the road to a deal. Much can happen to derail your deal between the heads of agreement and the completion. For this reason, we generally suggest that owners do not reveal the heads of agreement or the proposed deal to customers, suppliers or employees (except on a 'need to know' basis). There will be plenty of time for jubilation once you have cemented the deal.

8

The sale and purchase agreement and completion of the deal

There is an old saying in the merger business: 'A deal is never done until you have received the cash.' How true that is! The entire process is dynamic, constantly in flux until the day of completion. 'There is many a slip between cup and lip.'

Once you have negotiated a price, structure and terms, and have then recorded the heads of agreement, you are on the home stretch. But you cannot give up the race at this point. You still have two vital legs to run before the race is over: presiding over the buyer's due diligence process and negotiating and executing the sale and purchase agreement. The two processes generally occur simultaneously, primarily because it is in everyone's best interest to complete an agreed deal as soon as possible.

Unlike wine, deals do not age well; they tend to get stale with time. The longer it takes to complete a deal, the more time buyers have to rethink or renege on their obligations. As time drags on, there is also an increasing likelihood that word will leak out. Time generally hurts sellers more than buyers, especially with regard to customers or employees, so remain diligent about pushing your deal along.

Once a heads of agreement has been executed, it is customary for both sides to agree to a 45–90 day time frame to complete a deal. You can always extend the period if need be, but it is important for you to keep the time pressure on the buyer (as well as your accountants and legal advisers), lest nothing will proceed as scheduled.

You should also remember that even though you have generally agreed to a deal, negotiations are never over until a deal closes. You still have to go through the process of producing a mutually acceptable sale and purchase agreement, which involves its own set of negotiations. In addition, there are certain buyers who will wait until the day of completion before attempting to renegotiate a deal, counting on easy capitulation from sellers already committed to a transaction. Of course, you should never be overly suspicious or cautious. Still, you should remain diligent throughout the process and never let your guard slip.

Due diligence

Buyers generally make offers on your business based solely on information provided by you. Until the heads of agreement has been executed, buyers have no opportunity to either verify that the information provided to them was accurate and complete, or to otherwise engage in a diligent and thorough examination of the business that they are about to buy.

The term 'due diligence' has its genesis in the US Securities Act of 1933, which basically outlined methods to achieve 'full and fair disclosure' of all pertinent material facts relating to publicly held securities. The Act provided a general overview of the breadth and depth of information that companies must provide to investors so that those parties can engage in proper 'due diligence' prior to investing. In the market for private companies, 'due diligence' has come to refer to the process by which a prospective buyer both verifies all previously provided data and also undertakes a full review of all other relevant information prior to legally committing to a deal. While corporate raiders may initiate takeovers of large public companies without proper due diligence, it is rare that anyone will buy a smaller private company without a thorough examination of all aspects of the company before committing any money.

While each buyer will want to examine differing aspects of your business in differing degrees of detail, due diligence inquiries generally focus on the following broad areas:

- corporate structure and ownership;
- products, including the manufacturing process and markets;
- customers and suppliers;
- sales and marketing;
- production plant and equipment;
- management and employees;
- reporting and control systems;
- financial results and balance sheet;
- pension scheme(s);
- environmental issues;
- legal issues.

A detailed listing of a typical 'due diligence checklist' is provided in Appendix III.

More likely than not, a buyer will engage his lawyers to conduct a thorough study of your company's corporate documents and legal standing. A buyer will also probably engage his accounting firm to perform a full financial review, both to produce a closing balance sheet and to verify all past financial records.

While much of a buyer' s due diligence can take place at your accountant's or lawyer's office, it will be necessary for the buyer to conduct some of his examination at your premises. A buyer will certainly want the opportunity to fully inspect your physical plant. In addition, they will want to meet and interview your company's management, to get comfortable with both their operating abilities and their future commitment to the company.

It is unreasonable to deny access to your facilities or management during a due diligence period; on the other hand, by no means should a prospective buyer have open access to your company. The heads of agreement should outline in detail all due diligence procedures, which generally require that all factory visits and management interviews be arranged through you. It is customary that all due diligence occurs during business hours. To minimise exposure, however, you may want to arrange for some due diligence visits to occur after hours.

Due diligence is a necessary evil in getting a deal done. The process will become very tedious very quickly. You will undoubtedly tire of the endless requests for information or explanations of company practices.

Very little of your past or present operations will go uncovered or unnoticed. And yet, throughout the process, you need to keep in mind that you would probably go into just as much painful detail if you were buying your own company. After all, you have had years to understand the internal workings of your company; a prospective buyer has at best a few months to acquaint himself. You need to have the patience to educate your buyer as to all the mundane but vital details of your company.

The sale and purchase agreement

A sale and purchase agreement is a legal document which sets forth all of the agreements and understandings between the buyer and vendor of a business. The document not only covers the price, terms and structure of a deal, but it also details all of the other legal and financial aspects of the transaction. Unlike a heads of agreement, a sale and purchase agreement is legally binding; a party to the agreement that fails to perform is liable for damages.

As with the heads of agreement, it is customarily the buyer's responsibility to draft the sale and purchase agreement. While this may appear unfair, there is a certain logic to it. A sale and purchase agreement is basically written for the protection of the buyer. After all, a seller walks away from a deal with cash. The buyer's only source of recourse for fraud or misrepresentation is the sale and purchase agreement.

None the less, the drafting of the sale and purchase agreement constitutes an enormous advantage for the buyer; he not only gets to frame the initial document to favour his interests, but he also has the opportunity to add points or conditions not previously negotiated.

We have never been involved with a sale and purchase agreement that has not undergone several rounds of substantial redrafting before a mutually acceptable document is produced.

The negotiation of the sale and purchase document essentially picks up where the negotiations of the heads of agreement stopped. Copies of the tables of contents of two sale and purchase agreements, one for a share deal and the other for an asset deal, are provided in Appendices IV and V. In general, most acquisition agreements cover the following areas.

The price, terms and structure of the deal

Most sale and purchase agreements commence with what is generally considered the most important feature of the document: a detailed description of the price, terms and structure of the transaction.

The first issue to be addressed is generally the structure of the deal: whether the deal will take the form of a share sale, an asset transaction, a recapitalisation or a merger. In the case of an asset transaction, the document must include full details of exactly what assets are being sold; what assets, if any, are being excluded; and what specific liabilities are being assumed by the buyer.

The price is generally expressed as either a fixed amount (say '£16 million') or a formula ('the selling company's net worth plus £10 million'). Typically, formulas are used when the purchase price is pegged to the selling company' s balance sheet as of the completion date. The deal is completed based on an estimated balance sheet, with post-completion adjustments made after the preparation of a final completion balance sheet.

This section of the document also identifies and explains in detail all of the terms that constitute the purchase price, including cash, loan notes, shares or contingent payments.

Representations and warranties

Representations and warranties refer to binding claims each party makes with respect to their company and the transaction. In this section of the sale and purchase agreement, both the buyer and the vendor warrant certain claims to each other.

Buyers' representations are generally limited to the fact that they are legally and financially able to make the acquisition.

Vendors' representations are generally much broader and far-reaching. Most vendors are called on to make detailed representations and warranties as to the nature and condition of their company, in addition to their legal ability to consummate the transaction.

Questions over the nature and extent of vendor representations are generally the most fertile ground for argument and negotiations between a buyer and a seller. After paying a fair price for a business, a buyer naturally wants some assurances as to the legal, financial and business aspects of the selling company. Almost without question, buyers will demand to be protected from contingent, undisclosed or unknown liabilities, such as outstanding litigation, environmental problems or unpaid taxes. Buyers logically argue that such liabilities may detract from the value of the business – had they been aware of such liabilities at the outset, they would have offered a commensurably lower amount. Thus, buyers want a mechanism to be compensated for any undisclosed or unknown liabilities that existed at the time of the closing. (This is not to be confused with buyers wanting protection from ordinary business risk. No one expects sellers to warrant against business failure caused by inept management, competition, a loss of customers, or a downturn in the economy.)

Representations and warranties are intended to set forth both parties' mutual understanding of the selling company. Through this exercise, buyers will ostensibly have a full understanding and assurance as to what they are buying.

Most sellers attempt to sell their company 'as is', shunning any on-going exposure in the future. However, rarely will a buyer proceed on a transaction where he cannot get a minimum of representations and warranties from a seller.

It is typical for vendors to at least warrant the following:

- The selling company is in good standing and has good and marketable title to all assets and properties. The company has all required licences and permits to conduct its business and is not in violation of any regulatory codes.
- All contract rights and leases are in good standing and not in threat of being terminated.
- No litigation exists or is pending against the company (except as specified).
- There are no liens or encumbrances on any of the company assets (except as specified).
- All financial statements fairly and accurately present the company's financial condition and recent performance.
- All required tax returns have been filed, and all tax payments due have been paid.
- There are no liabilities other than those that the vendor has detailed in the various schedules and exhibits of the sale and purchase agreement.

Since you know the most about your company, you are the one who should be in the best position to understand the risks associated with each of the representations and warranties demanded by a buyer. Your refusal to provide a specific warranty may cause buyers to become wary.

Still, it is to your advantage to eliminate or very narrowly define the warranties you have to make regarding your company. The fewer and more specific the representations and warranties, the less exposure you have to claims for damages after completion. You are able to reduce your exposure by listing in a disclosure letter any items of which you are aware, and thus bringing them to the buyer's attention before the deal is completed.

Covenants

The completion of a deal often occurs simultaneously with the signing of the sale and purchase agreement. However, for a number of reasons, completion can occur after the actual signing of the agreement.

Buyers may want to quickly sign an agreement for specific tax or accounting reasons, leaving the fine details of actually completing the deal to a later date. The covenants section of the sale and purchase agreement outlines the obligations of each party during the period between the signing and completion.

While some covenants pertain to the buyer's conduct during this period (such as the maintenance of confidentiality), most are directed at the seller. These covenants protect the buyer from major changes in the legal, financial or business aspects of the selling company pending completion.

Sellers are generally obliged to carry on in the normal course of business, undertaking no new projects and incurring no new indebtedness or extraordinary expenditures, including bonuses or dividends. Indeed, most covenants are aimed at maintaining the status quo at the selling company.

The logic behind these covenants is obvious: once you have agreed to sell the shares of your company for £10 million, a buyer wants to protect against you pulling a £2 million dividend out of the company just before completion, making the de facto cost to the buyer grow to £12 million.

Covenants can be either affirmative or negative; that is, they can either demand that you do something (like maintain a certain net worth) or not do something (like take a dividend). Negative covenants are termed such because they prohibit sellers from acts that would diminish the value of the business.

Most buyers will insist on some form of non-compete as a part of the overall agreement. As discussed earlier, a covenant not to compete essentially prevents owners from directly or indirectly competing with their company once they have sold. In any deal, an acquirer is ostensibly buying both your tangible assets and your intangible assets – such as your way of doing business, your customer relationships and your technical or marketing know-how. Naturally, a buyer will want a mechanism to prevent competitors from obtaining those intangibles.

Non-compete clauses within employment contracts have to be reasonable in respect of time and location, and if widely worded can be difficult to enforce. However, non-compete clauses within the sale and purchase agreement are much more robust. The view is taken that it is reasonable for the buyer to be able to protect his investment, and the seller has been paid not to compete. Courts have displayed a willingness to enforce the restrictions of non-compete covenants as a part of the sale of a business.

Generally non-compete covenants cover a 3–5 year time frame; anything beyond that is generally considered unreasonable.

Most buyers will want to define the covenant as broadly as their lawyers will allow. You should certainly attempt to narrow the agreement to a workable arrangement. However, we have seen too many owners expend great time and effort in negotiating limitations on the non-compete, often causing quite a commotion in the process. If you sincerely have no intention of ever competing, or are selling to retire from business, it is far preferable to concede to a broadly defined non-compete in exchange for other points that are more important to you.

Conditions for completion

If the signing and completion do not occur simultaneously, most purchase agreements include a section outlining the conditions precedent for completion. This section lists conditions under which either the buyer or the seller has the right to terminate the agreement without being liable for damages. If all of these conditions are met, then both parties are obligated to complete. Of course, even if certain conditions are not met, both sides can mutually agree to proceed with the deal anyway.

Typical conditions to a deal are the clearance of the transaction by the Inland Revenue, or by regulatory agencies, the satisfactory financing of the deal, and the transference of a lease. In addition, buyers will want to make certain that you are conforming with all of the affirmative and negative covenants before completion.

Because the conditions precedent are typically for the benefit of the buyer, you need to make certain that all conditions are reasonable and specific. Before you sign any 'conditional' agreement, you must soberly assess the sincerity and ability of the buyer to complete the transaction. The last thing that you want is to be bound by an open-ended, conditional agreement, which amounts to giving the buyer an 'option' on your company. After all, the seller generally has little control over many of the conditions, such as the buyer securing satisfactory financing.

You should very narrowly specify both the number and the breadth of any conditions, in addition to imposing a strict deadline for the buyer to satisfy those conditions.

Indemnities

The indemnity section of the sale and purchase agreement establishes the liability of each party for problems that are discovered after the closing. This section essentially outlines the circumstances and procedures under which either party can claim damages in the event of a breach of the representations or warranties.

As with most other sections of the sale and purchase document, the indemnity section is primarily for the protection of the buyer. Buyers will generally insist that you indemnify them for problems that arise from a breach of representations and warranties after completion. This is only fair. After all, an acquirer will buy your company based on certain representations. If things are not as you portrayed them, buyers understandably want some recourse.

While a buyer would probably be able to take legal action against a seller in the event of fraud or misrepresentation anyway, the indemnity section clearly and succinctly defines the procedures under which a buyer can come after you to recover damages.

Of course, this section typically contains cross-indemnification; the buyer agrees to indemnify you in the event of a breach of his representations and warranties, however slight that possibility is.

The duration of an indemnity is generally a major point of contention. Without a specific provision setting a time frame, it is possible that the representations and warranties may not 'survive' past completion. However, most buyers insist on at least a 2–3 year 'window' during which sellers are fully liable for all breaches of general warranties. Because the Inspector of Taxes can go back for 6 years into the affairs of a company, the tax deed and warranties are often required to be indemnified for a period of 7 years.

Another issue to address with regard to seller indemnities is the total aggregate amount of exposure a seller has to buyer claims. Buyers will usually want indemnities up to the amount they have paid for the company. However, because most major issues are uncovered in due diligence, we have found buyers can be negotiated into accepting a limit to seller exposure at a fraction of the purchase price (generally of the order of 50 per cent). This gives the seller some comfort that not all the consideration is 'at risk', and yet still provides a buyer with the knowledge that significant funds are available for unforeseen breaches or problems.

Rarely do transactions involving private companies not eventually produce some breaches of warranties. From the uncollectability of some debtors to a contractual commitment gone sour, it is almost a certainty that some problems will arise during the 'survival' period.

Sellers have a legitimate concern about being held accountable for a series of small, immaterial claims by the buyer. Thus it is customary for both parties to establish a mechanism where sellers are only liable for claims based on significant problems, or where minor breaches aggregate to significant problems.

The typical solution to this dilemma is to establish a 'basket'. A basket is a minimum threshold which must be reached, singularly or in the aggregate, before a seller's liability is triggered. By establishing a basket, a buyer cannot seek to recover damages unless and until total claims meet a certain, pre-set aggregate amount. A basket shields a seller from dealing with innumerable petty claims, while at the same time protecting the buyer from suffering serious damage.

Baskets typically range from 1 to 2 per cent of the total purchase price, or are, say, £125,000 on a £12.5 million transaction. Baskets generally work in one of two ways: either the seller is liable for the entire amount of the damages once the basket has been 'tipped', or he is liable for only those claims above the basket threshold. (In other words, in a situation with a £200,000 basket and £400,000 of claims, the first scenario would leave the seller liable for the full £400,000, while the second scenario would limit his exposure to only the excess £200,000.) Of course, the mechanism and threshold of the basket are subject to negotiation. Expect buyers to initially refuse to even consider a basket, though most end up capitulating to the notion.

No buyer wants to face the unenviable task of attempting to retrieve a part of the purchase price from a seller. This becomes especially difficult when the seller was paid in cash and has either squandered the money or has moved to some far-away country. To protect their interests and make certain that there will be adequate funds available to satisfy their claims, most buyers will insist on putting a portion of the purchase consideration in an escrow account for the duration of the indemnification.

In an all-cash deal, you should be prepared for a buyer to insist on an escrow. An escrow account is the buyer's only real assurance that money will be around to satisfy his claims. The amount of the escrow is generally dependent on how comfortable the buyer is with the strength and veracity of your representations and warranties. By no means, however, should you allow an escrow to amount to more than 20 per cent of the purchase consideration (the percentage gets smaller as the deal size increases). All escrow accounts should be interest-bearing and should be administered by a third party.

We typically attempt to arrange for an increasing percentage of the escrow to be released to the seller as time passes and the threat of major misrepresentation lessens. Under no circumstances should the escrow extend beyond the duration of the indemnification.

In a transaction that involves a significant deferred payout, such as a loan note or an earn-out, an escrow becomes less vital to a buyer. In the event that significant damages do arise in such circumstances, buyers generally establish their claims against those deferred payments. In essence, those payments act as the escrow.

Completion

Completion is the actual event at which a transaction is consummated through the execution of all documentation and the transfer of title or shares in exchange for a like transfer of funds.

In most instances, the completion day will be as hectic and chaotic as any you will have ever encountered. Every group that is a party to the deal will be at the completion, along with their respective advisers. There may be dozens of people involved with the actual completion: from you and the buyer, to the buyer's financiers and your bankers. This, of course, can cause a logistical as well as an administrative nightmare. The buyer's legal team will generally be responsible for coordinating all of the documentation and the sequence of events.

You should be certain that all documents are negotiated, reviewed and approved well before the day of completion. Completion *should* be a mere formality. You do not want to let the buyer have any opportunity to renegotiate the deal or wangle out of any obligations.

Well in advance of the completion day, your lawyer should provide you with the litany of documents you will need to bring to the completion, including the share certificates, articles of incorporation, company minute book and tax records, to name but a few. In addition, you need to give yourself and your advisers adequate time to compile and prepare all necessary exhibits, disclosures, schedules and other information you will need for the sale and purchase document.

We were recently involved with a seller whose lack of foresight and planning in these matters caused him to lose a deal. The seller owned a clothing company which marketed its products under various brand names. Both he and the buyer thought all the names were trademarked – obviously a very important factor in protecting the brands. The seller's lawyer fell behind in preparing various disclosures to the purchase document. Rather than delay the closing, both sides agreed to review the missing exhibits on the day of the closing. Unfortunately, one of these exhibits was the documentation relating to the trademarks. To our client's surprise and the buyer's dismay, one of the brands was not trademarked – it was free to be used by any manufacturer.

The buyer was more upset by the fact that the seller did not have a grasp on his business than the fact that the brand was not trademarked. Clearly, the buyer must have wondered what other troubling aspects of the business went unnoticed or unknown by the seller.

There is no doubt that if our client had coordinated the compilation of the exhibits in a more organised manner, he would have discovered the problem well before completion day and would have had time to deal with it. The element of surprise, more than anything else, killed the deal.

It is important to remember that you are not just executing documents at completion; you are also transferring your entire business to another party. It is advisable to meet with your legal team a few times before completion so that you are familiar with all of the various documents and your obligations at completion.

Most acquisitions require cash payments to be made by bank transfer. We always advise that the funds are transferred into the buyer's solicitor's client account the day before completion. In that way you know the funds exist, and your solicitor can obtain a binding commitment from the buyer's solicitor to transfer the funds.

Many owners have told us that they find the pressures and anxiety of the completion process to be extremely stressful. None the less, it is important to keep some perspective on the matter. After all, the completion is the culmination of a long and arduous process; completion will also bring with it a tremendous amount of exhilaration, relief and, best of all, money.

9 *Case study: Advanced Technologies Ltd*

Perhaps the clearest way to summarise all the points we have raised in this book is to present a case study of a company that recently went through the process of selling. This study will succinctly demonstrate how the selling process works, in addition to highlighting the trials and tribulations inherent in any sale of a business. In order to protect our client's privacy, we have changed the names of the companies and individuals involved, as well as modified the description of the company's operations. No reference is intended to any company with a name similar to the fictitious names used here. The story, however, remains representative of the process.

Description of the company and brief history

Advanced Technologies Ltd manufactures a proprietary line of aluminium castings for the automotive and business machine industries. Located in the West Midlands, the company is a recognised leader in its field and has established a strong reputation for the quality of its products and its innovative approach to engineering problems.

Advanced was founded in 1973 by James Smith, when he was 55 years old. Soon afterwards, his only son, Chris, joined the company. By 1985, Chris had assumed the role of Managing Director, as his father began to spend more of his time in Portugal. By 1990, the company had grown to over £5 million of annual sales, and James Smith had gifted all of his shares in equal proportions to his son, Chris, and his three daughters.

In 1998, Chris Smith saw a need for a stronger management team to guide the company into the future. After an exhaustive search, he hired an operations Director, Tom Ward, who had extensive experience running a large division of a FTSE 100 company in a similar industry. Tom Ward was attracted to Advanced because of its superior reputation and its growth potential. Another, even greater, attraction was that Chris Smith was 62 and nearing retirement age. At 45, Tom Ward was hired with the explicit understanding that he would become the MD within three years and was given share options, based on the then current value of the company.

Tom Ward had an immediate impact on the company. He expanded the product offerings into new fields and introduced more efficient production techniques to the plant. Tom also knew how to delegate responsibility, and he soon began to recruit a strong second-tier of management to back him up. Most importantly, Tom was able to introduce change without disrupting the company's steady growth or profitability.

In 2000, Chris Smith retired, and Tom Ward assumed the MD'S role. The company continued to grow and prosper under Tom's tutelage. A summary of its financial performance is provided in Table 9.1:

Table 9.1 Operating results – Advanced Technologies Ltd

	Actual (£000)				Projected (£000)
	FYE 31/12/1998	FYE 31/12/1999	FYE 31/12/2000	FYE 31/12/2001	31/12/2002
Net sales	£20,100	£24,700	£27,400	£30,600	£35,000
CAGR	–	22.8%	10.9%	11.7%	14.4%
Gross profit	£6,210	£7,780	£8,900	£9,730	£11,200
Gross margin	30.9%	31.5%	32.5%	31.8%	32.0%
Profit before tax and discretionary costs*	£2,210	£2,840	£3,425	£3,670	£4,200
Profit before tax	£1,610	£2,240	£2,825	£3,070	£3,600

FYE = Fiscal year ending; CAGR = Compound annual growth rate
* Includes salaries and directors' fees paid to members of the Smith family

The company also had a strong balance sheet, as the Smith family had a policy of reinvesting most of the company's earnings back into the company. The balance sheet is summarised below, as of the fiscal year ending 31 December 2001:

Table 9.2   Balance sheet – Advanced Technologies Ltd

	31/12/2001 £000	£000
Intangible assets		£250
Fixed assets		
Property and equipment	£9,870	
Accumulated depreciation	£3,730	
Net fixed assets		£6,140
Current assets	£9,395	
Current liabilities	£4,685	
Net current assets		£4,710
Long-term liabilities		£(2,650)
Net assets		£8,450
Share capital and reserves		£8,450

Day 1: 4 January 2002

In keeping with tradition, the Smith family held its annual Board meeting just after the Christmas holidays. As Managing Director, Tom Ward presided over the meeting. He reviewed the company's performance in 2001 and its prospects for the new year. Tom foresaw a great future for the company. Indeed, just a few months earlier, two potential customers had approached Tom about significant new business opportunities, both of which would commence by 2Q 2002. Yet, to capitalise on these opportunities and to generally stay competitive, Tom was convinced that it was going to be necessary to spend £3.5 million over the next two years to expand the factory. The company had a strong balance sheet and could afford to borrow the money.

Janet Klein, Chris Smith's eldest sister, looked visibly startled. Each sibling had been receiving £150,000 a year as a Director's fee. She explained that she had planned to petition the Board for an increased payment. Now that her husband was retired, she counted on this income to support them. Her youngest daughter had decided to return to university, and Mrs Klein had plans to buy a small weekend house. Suddenly, her income from the company was not enough.

Several of the other siblings also expressed an interest in increasing their income from the company. Tom Ward explained that cash flow would be very tight if the expansion plans were carried out and that the family's income would more probably have to be decreased, not increased.

After the question of expansion versus income was briefly debated, Chris Smith put forward the idea of selling the company. Just a few months earlier, he had received an unsolicited approach from a Leeds-based investment group called Charles Holdings. Chris explained that as no family member was still involved in the company, a move like this would probably not upset their 83-year-old father too much.

Perhaps selling was the answer to their dilemma: it would allow the shareholders their liquidity, without burdening the company's expansion plans. After some discussion, the rest of the family appeared quite interested in exploring this matter. Tom Ward was given the mandate to investigate and report back to the family.

Day 12: 15 January 2002

Tom Ward had spent the past few days compiling information on advisers to help the family explore this issue further. He had narrowed his list down to three candidates: the corporate finance division of his local bank, a specialist corporate finance boutique and our firm. On 15 January Tom called our office. He said we had been recommended by a former client and invited us to visit him and look at his operation.

After reviewing the company's financial statements and marketing materials, and doing some outline research into the market, we travelled to the Midlands to see Tom and visit the company.

Day 15: 18 January 2002

We drove to the main factory, where we were to spend the day. As we came into the office, Tom met us and casually announced to the receptionist that we were a consulting firm that he had hired to do some market research for the company. This remained our 'cover identity' for the entire time we worked for the company.

We spent the next hour walking through the factory and were very pleased with what we saw. The plant was clean, and the employees appeared to be hard working. There were many efficiency awards displayed, as well as letters of excellence from customers. The next few hours were spent reviewing the company's history, current performance and future prospects. We also discussed all the elements we would need to prepare the information memorandum, should the company decide to appoint us.

During a late lunch, we met Chris Smith and Janet Klein, Chris Smith's sister. After some brief conversation, we got down to the crux of the matter: they were interested in what we thought the business was worth.

Fortunately, prior to the meeting, Tom had provided us with five years of historical statements, as well as three years of projections. We reviewed with Chris Smith and his sister the current state of the market, and the specific prospects for the company going forward. We concluded that we believed that a 6–6.5 multiple of projected, re-constructed FY 2002 pre-tax profits could be achieved (after tax P/E of 8.5–9.0), assuming we were able to create an active market for the company. This equated to a value of £24–27 million. As importantly, we discussed the value below which they would (should) not sell, and agreed this would be £21 million.

After lunch we had a brief tour of the company's adjacent unit before departing. Tom Ward told us he would be in touch with us in the next two weeks.

Day 26: 29 January 2002

Tom had called us several days earlier to say that his personal choice was for us to represent the company, but that the ultimate decision rested with the Board. He wanted us to meet the Board to make a presentation. We accepted the invitation and, on the afternoon of 29 January we met with the entire Board: Chris Smith and his three sisters.

After introducing ourselves, we gave a brief history of our firm and discussed our operating philosophy and approach to the market. We handed out references of several owners whose firms we had recently sold. Next, we discussed the company's prospects. We presented our valuation range and explained how we had arrived at it.

We turned then to the most important part of the meeting: a general discussion of how all the shareholders felt about selling the company. Although we had ostensibly been invited to the Board meeting after a decision to sell had already been made, we knew from prior experience that, more likely than not, there was no unanimity of opinion. As it turned out, the situation with Advanced Technologies was no exception.

Anne James, the youngest sibling, was very much against selling altogether. She was a very successful estate agent, married to an entrepreneur, who clearly did not need the income she received from the company. She felt that the company was part of the family, and that selling it would be like selling a part of themselves. Besides, as a major employer in the area, the company provided the entire family with a certain amount of prestige.

Janet Klein had had several weeks to think about selling the company since the matter had come up at the annual Board meeting. She owned 25 per cent of the shares (23.75 per cent after allowing for Tom's options). If the company was worth as much as £25 million, she would receive £6 million pre-tax. Investing that amount in government bonds would yield over £250,000 in annual income – significantly more than she was getting now. Furthermore, the return was guaranteed and not predicated on the good fortune of the company. Alternatively, her capital would be made liquid, free to be spent if she so chose. She and her husband were very interested in selling.

Beth Kellogg, the middle daughter, and her husband were both teachers. While they enjoyed having the income from the company, they lived a rather modest life, and in fact saved most of their discretionary income. Beth was indifferent regarding the sale. She believed that it would be easier from an estate perspective if her holdings in the company were liquid. However, since she was only 55 and in good health, she was not too concerned about this matter. The one point that did matter to her was that she did not want the sale of the company to divide the family. She could already see the battle lines being drawn between Anne and Janet.

Like his sister Janet, Chris Smith realised that his income would increase dramatically by selling the company. But, like his sister Anne, he knew it would be difficult for him to participate in the sale of the business his father had started.

However, Chris had another, larger problem on his mind. His wife, Caroline, had heard a rumour from some mutual friends that Tom Ward had recently been offered the position of MD of a much larger company. Chris was quite aware that Tom had become essential to the company's future and, therefore, the value of the business. It was Tom who engineered the tremendous growth in revenues and profitability over the previous five years. Chris was not at all certain that he could return to run the company should Tom leave. Even if he could, he had absolutely no desire to return from his comfortable retirement to do so. Chris Smith realised that he *should* pursue a sale, if only to continue to provide Tom Ward with a stimulating and challenging work environment.

For an hour, each of the siblings presented their points of view. The discussion went round and round with no resolution being reached. Finally, Anne suggested they call their father, who, after all, had started the company. Although James Smith was now in his 80s, his mind was still very quick. We left the room while the siblings called their father in Portugal. Much to everyone's surprise, James Smith was quite determined that the company be sold. He saw a sale as the one way to adequately secure the future for all his children and grandchildren. That, more than just the company, would be his legacy.

Just as important to James Smith, however, were the advantages of a sale to both Advanced Technologies and Tom Ward. James Smith felt strongly that no company could stand still and remain competitive. The family either had to commit to fund the continued expansion of Advanced, or decide to sell. It was unfair to both James Smith, who had founded the company, and Tom Ward, who had truly built the company, to hold it back.

We were summoned back to the meeting and given the mandate to sell the company. Our agreement stated that we would represent Advanced Technologies on an exclusive basis for nine months. We left Tom Ward with a list of items we would need in order to prepare the information memorandum.

Day 43: 15 February 2002

Tom Ward had sent the information we had requested within the week and by 15 February we had a working first draft of the memorandum.

We had also prepared an initial list of 60 potential acquirers whom we wanted to approach. This list was narrowed down from a larger universe of 350 parties we deemed as likely candidates. These potential buyers included European and American firms, large domestic companies in related fields and a few well-capitalised private investment groups. The list did not include any companies who were direct competitors. Our goal was to keep the process confidential and to handle the approaches with discretion. A separate list of competitors was drawn up. The family and we could decide at a later date whether to approach these parties.

Day 50: 22 February 2002

We were now on the third and final draft of the information memorandum. The list had been reviewed, and three parties had been excluded, because Tom Ward had had personal dealings with each of these firms and was not comfortable with their management styles.

We began to make discreet direct approaches to the potential buyers on the list. We contacted the appropriate person at each company and discussed their acquisition goals. If the conversation sounded promising, we described our client in general terms, without providing any specifics. We only released detailed information after a confidentiality letter had been agreed and signed.

Of the 57 companies we approached, 25 were interested in receiving more information. After they signed the confidentiality letters, we provided them with the information memorandum.

While we were pleased with our initial response rate (44 per cent), our goal was to send out at least 40 memoranda. From our first set of calls, it appeared that the parties most interested in Advanced Technologies were those in related fields, so we returned to our initial universe of potential suitors and chose an additional 40 parties to approach.

From this second group of candidates, an additional 20 companies (50 per cent) requested the information memorandum.

Day 68: 12 March 2002

Of the 45 companies that received the information, five had already returned it. One was not interested because they did not like the company's concentration of customers in the automotive field. Another discovered from the report that the company had a union, a definite negative to them.

By this point, we had been in touch with all of the suitors that had received the report. Several had requested some additional information, many had only reviewed the report once and were not ready to comment, and a few were interested in visiting Tom Ward and examining the facilities. In order to avoid too many visits, we prepared a short video of the plant which Tom would talk through.

We arranged the first meeting for 12 March; Tom Ward met us and David Wilding, the Chairman of International Stamping, Inc at our offices. International Stamping was a £400 million manufacturer of various metal components, with headquarters in Detroit. In 1998, International Stamping had made an acquisition of another UK firm with a complementary product line. They had been pleased with their first British acquisition and were eager to continue expanding in the UK.

Tom took Daniel Wilding through the video in detail. He seemed visibly impressed with what he saw and complimented Tom on his operation. David Wilding had prepared a list of questions he wanted to review, which he had forwarded to us before the meeting. Tom had compiled a very impressive presentation which addressed all of Wilding's questions. In general, Tom was very responsive, direct and cooperative, as well as being enthusiastic.

After the meeting, we were convinced that the day had gone well. Tom was a positive seller, who was able to present the company in its best possible light. David Wilding confirmed our perceptions; he said that he would definitely get back to us with an offer. He inquired whether other companies were interested in buying Advanced, as he had a policy against getting involved in bidding wars. We assured him that he was the first to meet Tom, and that no one else had made an offer.

Day 82: 26 March 2002

True to his word, David Wilding called us a couple of weeks after his visit and made a verbal offer of £20 million. We were disappointed. Not only did we believe the total offer to be low, but only £17 million of the bid was for cash. Of the remaining £3 million, £2 million was to be paid as loan notes over five years, with the final £1 million to be paid at the end of two years if Advanced's profits grew at a 15 per cent rate over that period. Using a 10 per cent discount rate, we valued the £3 million future payments to be worth only a little more than £2 million. Hence, if the shareholders were to receive all of the future payments, the total equated to a present value of £19 million.

We responded to Wilding that we thought the offer was low. However, we did suggest that he put the offer in writing, and we would take it to the family. Wilding was quite accommodating, but instructed us that he was not interested in having his deal shopped around. He wanted a quick response.

We recognised that this was going to be a problem. The prior week, William Clark had visited the company and was excited about expanding into Advanced's product lines. Clark was the Chairman of Lindsay Industries, an AIM-listed, Peterborough-based manufacturer of plastic and metal components, with revenues of £275 million. Furthermore, we had three other companies scheduled to meet us over the next three weeks. While we certainly were not going to play by Wilding's rules, we did have to be careful in how we handled the matter going forward. After a conference with Tom Ward, we decided to suspend the search for more parties and concentrate instead on creating a market from those parties currently examining Advanced. If the market fizzled out, we could always go back to the well.

Day 103: 16 April 2002

Three weeks had passed since David Wilding had made his initial offer. Shortly after he presented his letter of intent, we responded that the family felt the total offer was too low and that the deal structure left too much of the purchase price on the back-end. Wilding countered that he would increase the cash by £1 million. After a few days wait, we once again told him that the offer was too low. He responded by increasing the cash by an additional £1 million, but added that the offer was his final one and would be outstanding only until 20 April. He sensed we were stalling for time, and he was right.

Meanwhile, after some discreet negotiating, Lindsay Industries had also made an offer. They proposed a share for share exchange, valuing Advanced at £26 million. Lindsay's share price had shown steady but consistent growth, and paid a 3 per cent dividend. An attractive feature of this offer was that, as a share deal, the shareholders could defer any tax liability until they sold their Lindsay shares. If they sold only a portion of the Lindsay shares, they would be taxed only on that portion.

Three other parties had visited over the past two weeks. A well-capitalised investor group, with a similar casting operation in Shef-field, had visited two weeks earlier. They seemed impressed at the meeting, but later called to say that Advanced was not a good fit with their operation. We were quite surprised, as Tom Ward believed that the two businesses truly complemented each other.

Herbert Orvis of Charles Holdings, the investment group that originally approached Chris Smith and acted as a catalyst to the entire matter, called Chris again. Chris put them in touch with us, and they too had spent a day with Tom examining the business.

Finally, Canam, a large, private diversified French company visited. The President of Canam's castings division, Francois Blanc, was very complimentary about the company in general and Tom Ward in particular. Canam wanted to expand into the UK. They had already looked at several British companies, but none had been up to their standards. François Blanc felt that they could bring a lot to Advanced, and that Advanced would offer them an ideal entree into the UK market. However, the decision was not his to make; the Chairman of Canam had the final say, as he owned and had an active interest in it. The Chairman could not visit the company for at least two weeks.

Day 123: 6 May 2002

Canam's chairman had spent the day with Tom Ward about two weeks after François Blanc's visit. Tom had been very impressed with him and had agreed to visit Canam's castings operation in France. François Blanc remained upbeat, but still had not made an offer. When pressured, he would put us off. 'Take another offer if you must', he would say. 'This is a big decision for us, and we must be certain it is the right one.' We decided to retreat from pressing too hard for fear he would walk.

Meanwhile we had gone back to David Wilding at International Stamping plc and told him we had an offer for £26 million. We did not mention that the offer was from Lindsay or that it was in shares. Naturally, Wilding was upset. However, he did not drop his offer, as he had threatened to do, but rather he increased it to £25 million in cash, with £3 million in loan notes paid at the end of five years. Using a 10 per cent discount rate, this offer was worth approximately £27 million.

Charles Holdings remained interested in Advanced, but they had a problem coming up with the cash. Because they were going to borrow a substantial portion of the purchase price, they could only arrange a cash payment of £18 million. Having been told of the offer for £26 million, Herbert Orvis of Charles claimed that they could top our best offer by £1.0 million. They offered the following: £18 million in cash; £5 million in seven-year notes paying 10 per cent interest; and a £3.0 million contingent payment to be paid at the end of three years if the company met certain earnings tests. In addition, they offered to let Tom and the family keep a 10 per cent ownership in the company.

Tom Ward was resolutely against selling to Charles. He recognised that the investment group might make the family the highest offer. However, by leveraging the balance sheet, they would also impair Ward's ability to expand his operations. The next five years would be spent concentrating on paying the debt, not growing the company. Despite his reservations about Charles, Tom accepted the fact that the decision was ultimately the family's, and he kept his opinions to himself.

Day 130: 13 May 2002

We had reached the day of reckoning. We had two good offers from groups that both Tom Ward and the family felt would take the company forward and help continue its growth. Both International Stamping and Lindsay were pressing us for an answer. We also had the offer from Charles Holdings, which was for a higher nominal value and had an added benefit of allowing the family to keep an interest in the company.

However, Tom felt that Canam was such a strong potential partner that he did not want the family to make a decision without hearing from them. At Tom's urging, we called François at Canam. We mentioned that we did not want to force his hand, but that the family had several other offers and were being pressed to take one. François asked us what our best offer was. We told him that there was a bid of £27 million, not mentioning the structure. He responded that he would call us back.

That afternoon, François Blanc called. He stated that Canam was pleased to offer £30 million in cash for Advanced. He further said he was not interested in negotiating, that his bid was more than fair, especially given the considerable additional investment that would be required to grow Advanced. In fact, François said that Canam was only willing to pay such a high price because the company was very well run and offered Canam a unique opportunity to get into the UK market.

After telling the family of the Canam offer, we immediately called David Wilding at International Stamping, as well as Herb Orvis at Charles Holdings and William Clark at Lindsay. Herb Orvis and David Wilding could do no better. However, William Clark said he was prepared to revise his offer subject to board approval. He said that he would be back to us by the end of the day. At around 6:00 pm, Clark called. He could offer £30 million in shares, but he demanded a final decision within two days.

Day 134: 17 May 2002

A special Board meeting of Advanced Technologies had been called to discuss the offers. Each had its merits and deserved careful consideration. As the family members sat down at the table, we gave them a sheet which summarised the offers (Table 9.3).

Table 9.3 Summary of offers for Advanced Technologies Ltd – 17 May 2002

BIDDER	UPFRONT CASH/STOCK	MAXIMUM SUBSEQUENT PAYMENTS	MAXIMUM TOTAL PRESENT VALUE
INTL. STAMPING	£25 million cash	£3 million	£28 million
LINDSAY IND.	£30 million shares		£30 million
CHARLES HLDGS.	£18 million cash	£8 million	£26 million (1)
CANAM	£30 million cash		£30 million

(1) Shareholders also retain 10 per cent of company

All agreed that the International Stamping and Charles Holdings offers were not as good as the others, either in total value or structure. Anne James was tempted by Charles' offer because she liked the idea of keeping part of the company. But she realised the heavy debt burden would make it difficult to continue to grow the company. Everyone also rejected the 'back-end' contingent nature of the Charles offer.

Both the Lindsay and Canam offers were for the same amount; both were secured offers. The only real difference was the form of payment. Lindsay's share deal would allow the shareholders to defer taxes, perhaps indefinitely. Yet, it did concentrate all of their wealth in one share, providing no real diversity. There would also be constraints as to how many shares could be sold at any one time, and the dividend was only 3 per cent. After much discussion, all four family members declared themselves neutral. They asked Tom Ward for his thoughts.

Tom stated that either suitor would be acceptable to him. Both wanted to grow the company, and both were committed to supplying him with the resources to do so. However, he personally believed Canam's management style to be more in accord with his own. He felt much more comfortable with their managers and their approach to business. If it was his decision, he would choose Canam.

The family members voted one by one. . . all in favour of Canam. We were instructed to call François Blanc and accept the bid. As we left to do so, Anne James started to cry.

Day 155: 7 June 2002

We had been very pleased with how the selling process had worked thus far. The market generated several fine offers. Tom Ward was happy with the pending acquirer, and the offer was at the high end of our expected range. However, we had premonitions that the closing process was not to be a smooth one when, two weeks after agreeing to the deal, the family still had not signed the heads of agreement.

What had started out as a minor issue in the heads of agreement had escalated into a huge impasse. Canam had included a standard clause that the shareholders would warrant and thus indemnify Canam against any unknown and undisclosed liabilities that had occurred while they had owned the company. As we have discussed in Chapter 8, this is a customary and not unreasonable request by a buyer. No acquirer wants to be liable for unknown or undisclosed problems that surface after the sale.

For 20 years, both Chris Smith and the company had used a small, local firm of solicitors for all of their legal work. The firm specialised in property and family matters. When Bill Lam, the partner in charge, reviewed the heads of agreement, he protested strongly against the warranty clause. He argued that the shareholders should under no circumstances agree to indemnify off-balance sheet liabilities.

In an attempt to circumvent this impasse, Canam decided to start writing the purchase agreement, without executing a heads of agreement. They hoped that the Advanced shareholders (and their lawyer) would be more reasonable if they got further into the negotiating process. However, François Blanc and his lawyers were very irritated. They wondered if Advanced's lawyer had a hidden agenda and did not really want the family to sell. It was clearly evident that Advanced was an important client to Bill Lam's firm. François wondered whether Lam was creating an untenable roadblock merely to scuttle the deal and retain an important client.

Day 246: 6 September 2002

Matters went from bad to worse. Not only was Bill Lam finding more and more things wrong with what appeared to be a reasonable sale and purchase agreement, but the company's performance was slipping. One of

Advanced's large customers had not come through with a big order that Tom had anticipated. Tom had revised his projected FY 2002 reconstructed pre-tax profits from £4.2 million to £3.8 million.

Meanwhile, the warranty issue was still not resolved. François Blanc had agreed to limit the amount of potential liability to £10 million (at one-third the purchase price, a very unusual concession), and agreed to there being no escrow. Mr Lam was still arguing for no warranty whatsoever.

Both the family and we were more concerned about the earnings drop than the arguments over the sale and purchase agreement. We fully expected Canam to move to lower the price, given the drastic decrease in earnings and the fact that the deal reflected a healthy multiple of projected earnings already. To our surprise and relief, François did not try to renegotiate the deal. This, more than anything, evidenced Canam's deep desire to buy Advanced.

However, François Blanc did use the deterioration in earnings to his advantage. He came back to the family and claimed that he would not negotiate the deal any further until the family retained another firm of lawyers to help Mr Lam complete the deal.

While he did not want to remove their long-trusted lawyer, François insisted that the family also use a larger firm with specific experience in mergers and acquisitions. At this point, the family was getting irritated with Bill Lam. Chris Smith, who was spearheading the operation, saw no serious risk in the warranty. After all, it only covered liabilities which were undisclosed. The company had audited accounts and did not have any outstanding litigation or environmental problems. They were always open and forthright about how they ran their business, and had been equally so in the due diligence with Canam. In the end, he was actually relieved to be able to appoint another legal adviser, and immediately did so.

Day 267: 27 September 2002

In less than two weeks, all of the issues relating to the sale and purchase agreement were resolved. The family accepted the £10 million warranty exposure, and almost nine months after the family had started to think about selling, the deal was done.

At the close, Chris Smith was nostalgic. Afterwards, he made a brief speech to the employees and thanked them for their loyal service. Then he turned the programme over to François Blanc. François told everyone how excited he was about the company's prospects, and how pleased he was that Advanced was now part of the Canam family.

Postscript

We called Tom Ward six months after completion to see how business was faring. He sounded very upbeat. Canam had steered over £5.0 million of new business to him. They had also committed to fund a £4.0 million plant expansion in the new year. Because he was being paid a substantial bonus based on performance, Tom was quite excited about both his and Advanced's continuing prospects.

We also talked to Chris Smith a year later. While he felt a bit sad that his family no longer owned the company, he had bought a villa in Portugal, close to his father, was enjoying his new motor boat, and was about to fly to Australia for a six-week holiday. On reflection, Chris exclaimed that the sale worked out quite well indeed for both him and his sisters.

Appendix I: Sample confidentiality agreements

Confidentiality agreement 1

Letter from prospective purchaser
Addressed to prospective vendor and adviser

STRICTLY PRIVATE AND CONFIDENTIAL

To: Adviser
        200 New Road
        Any City AB12 3CD

and

        XYZ Limited (the 'Client') and its subsidiaries
        100 Industrial Road
        Any City AB12 4EF

Dear Sirs

XYZ LIMITED

1.1 In consideration of you disclosing or agreeing to disclose to us information (in whatever format and medium and whether written or oral) concerning the Client (the 'Restricted Information'), we undertake both to you and to the Client that we shall:

i   Treat the Restricted Information and any other information or documentation in whatever medium received, or prepared, by or for us which contains or reflects Restricted Information or any review thereof (together the 'Confidential Information') as being strictly private and confidential and shall use our best endeavours to maintain its status as such.

ii Use and apply the Confidential Information solely for the purposes of evaluating the businesses of [eg a group engaged in the distribution and supply of automotive glass and glass processing] carried on by the Client with a view to the acquisition of those businesses or the vendor's interest in those businesses (the 'Proposed Transaction'), and not for any other purpose (including but without limited to procuring any commercial advantage over the Client).

iii Not at any time disclose or otherwise make available any of the Confidential Information to any person other than:

a   those officers and employees of our and our parent company who reasonably require in the course of (and solely for the purpose of) evaluation of the Proposed Transaction to receive and consider the Confidential Information;

b   our professional advisers where necessary for the Proposed Transaction.

We agree that any such disclosure is on the basis that such officers and employees and advisers are first made aware of, and accept and agree to be bound by, the strict provisions of this undertaking, and we will use our reasonable endeavours to ensure that such officers and employees and advisers abide by such obligations.

iv Keep a record of each location at which Confidential Information is situated and of each person who is given access to Confidential Information and upon receipt of a written demand from yourselves return and/or procure the return of the Restricted Information (as reduced to a tangible form or medium) to yourselves together with all copies thereof and destroy or procure the destruction of all Confidential Information not reduced to writing or otherwise non-written form.

v Not disclose the fact that negotiations/discussions are taking place or have taken place concerning the Proposed Transaction or any of the terms or conditions thereof save to the persons mentioned in paragraphs iii (a) and (b) above.

vi Not except with your prior written consent reproduce the Confidential Information (whether in eye or machine readable format) other than for purposes detailed in paragraph ii above.

1.2 These undertakings do not apply to (a) information that is in, or (otherwise than by breach of this Undertaking) comes into, the public domain; (b) information required to be disclosed by law; (c) information already in our possession from a legitimate source; or (d) information that we obtain from a third party entitled to disclose it.

1.3 We confirm that the delivery to us of any information (including, without limitation, budgets and financial forecasts and projections which may form part of the Restricted Information) does not, and shall not be deemed to, constitute any representation/expression of opinion or warranty by anyone as to its accuracy or completeness. Nor shall it form the basis of any contract which may be concluded in respect of the Proposed Transaction. No one shall have any liability to us or our representatives resulting from the use of the information by us or our representatives except as may be expressly provided in any formal written agreement entered into to effect the Proposed Transaction.

1.4 We further confirm that we, and the officers, employees or other representatives of our company, will not use the Confidential Information to make contact or approaches of any kind to the staff, customers or suppliers of the Client without your prior knowledge and written consent.

1.5 We will not from the date hereof until one year from the termination of negotiations or completion of the Proposed Transaction between yourselves and us seek to entice away from the business of the Client any employee or officer of the Client who is identified as a result of our access to Restricted Information or our evaluation of the Proposed Transaction.

1.6 We will be responsible for any breach of any of the terms of this Undertaking by us or by any of our officers, agents, employees or advisers to whom we provide Confidential Information. We agree to notify you promptly upon becoming aware of the loss of or unauthorised disclosure of all or any part of the Confidential Information.

1.7 We acknowledge that damages may be a wholly inadequate measure of loss in the event of any breach of the terms of this Undertaking and accordingly agree that in such event you shall be entitled to seek specific enforcement of the terms hereof (by injunction or otherwise) on such terms as any Court with jurisdiction may deem just and proper.

1.8 We agree that any failure by you at any time to enforce or exercise any of your rights under this Undertaking will not be construed as a waiver of your right to enforce or exercise that right in future or other rights under this Undertaking at any time.

1.9 The Contracts (Rights of Third Parties) Act 1999 shall not apply to this Undertaking. No person who is not a party to this Agreement (including any employee, officer, agent, representative or subcontractor of either party) shall have the right (whether under the Contracts (Rights of Third Parties) Act 1999 or otherwise) to enforce any term of this Agreement which expressly or by implication confers a benefit on that person without both your and our express prior agreement in writing, which agreement must refer to this clause.

1.10 We acknowledge that you exclude liability (except in respect of death or personal injury due to your negligence or in respect of any fraudulent misrepresentation) for any loss or damage (whether arising under contract, or tort or otherwise) suffered or incurred by us as a result of the supply to us or the use by us of any of the Restricted Information, in particular as a result of any errors or inaccuracies in any Restricted Information whether such losses arise directly or indirectly from a breach of the use of the Restricted Information as defined above.

1.11 We shall upon request confirm to you by statutory declaration or in writing our compliance with the provisions of this Undertaking.

1.12 [We hereby acknowledge that none of the Client's proprietary rights in relation to the Restricted Information is transferred to us by virtue of this letter.]

1.13 This Undertaking is governed by and shall be construed in accordance with English Law.

1.14 Any disputes or claim arising under or in connection with this Undertaking shall be subject to the exclusive jurisdictions of the Courts of England and Wales.

Yours faithfully
for and on behalf of*

....
*[   ]

(PROSPECTIVE PURCHASER)

....
Date

....
*[   ]

(PROSPECTIVE PURCHASER)

....
Date

For and on behalf of the Client and its shareholders

....
*[   ]
Director
(PROSPECTIVE VENDOR)

....
Date

* PLEASE PRINT NAME OF COMPANY AND DIRECTOR SIGNING
ON BEHALF OF THE COMPANY

For and on behalf of Advisers

....
[   ]
Director

....
Date

Confidentiality agreement 2

ON NOTEPAPER OF SUPPLIER OF CONFIDENTIAL
INFORMATION, EG ADVISER/VENDOR

Our ref:
STRICTLY PRIVATE AND CONFIDENTIAL

[The Directors
Potential Purchaser]

Dear Sirs

ABC LIMITED

1.1 We understand that you wish to investigate the business of ABC
Limited [description of company eg 'our client, a North-West-based
printing company'] (the 'Company') [and of its subsidiaries] (together
the 'Group') [in connection with [insert nature of transaction, eg your
interest in acquiring the entire issued share capital of the company]
(the 'Permitted Purpose')] and that you, your directors and employees,
other potential syndicate members or [your/other] providers of finance
and your financial and professional advisers in relation to the Permitted
Purpose (together referred to as the 'Disclosees'), will need access to
certain information relating to the Company (the 'Confidential
Information') [including, without limitation, eg an Information
Memorandum prepared by Adviser].

1.2 In consideration of our agreeing to supply, and so supplying, the
Confidential Information to you [and agreeing to enter into discussions
with you] you hereby undertake and agree as follows:

  i   To hold the Confidential Information in confidence and not to
disclose or permit it to be made available to any person, firm or
company (except to other Disclosees), without our prior [written]
consent.

  ii Only to use the Confidential Information for the Permitted Purpose.

  iii To ensure that each Disclosee to whom disclosure of Confidential

Information is made by you is fully aware in advance of your obligations under this letter.

iv Upon written demand from us either to return the Confidential Information and any copies of it or to confirm to us in writing that, save as required by law or regulation, it has been destroyed. You shall not be required to return reports, notes or other material prepared by you or other Disclosees or on your or their behalf which incorporate Confidential Information ('Secondary Information') provided that the Secondary Information is kept confidential.

v To keep confidential and not reveal to any person, firm or company (other than Disclosees) the fact of your investigations into the Company or that discussions or negotiations are taking place or have taken place between us in connection with the proposed transaction or that potential acquirers are being sought for the Company.

vi That no person gives any warranty or makes any representation as to the accuracy or otherwise of the Confidential Information, save as may subsequently be agreed.

1.3 Nothing in paragraphs 1.2(i) to (vi) of this letter shall apply to any information or Confidential Information:

i which at the time of its disclosure is in the public domain;

ii which after disclosure comes into the public domain for any reason except your failure, or failure on the part of any Disclosee, to comply with the terms of this letter;

iii which was lawfully in your possession prior to such disclosure and is or becomes free from any restriction on its subsequent disclosure or use by you;

iv which is subsequently received by you from a third party without obligations of confidentiality; or

v which you or a Disclosee are required to disclose, retain or maintain by law or any regulatory or government authority.

1.4 Upon disclosure of the Company's identity to you, you and the officers of your company agree not to approach the following persons in relation to any of the Confidential Information disclosed to you, unless and until approval is given by us:

    i   customers, suppliers or any other third party to whom the Company are contracted;

    ii employees of the Company.

1.5 You agree that you will not visit [any of] the Company's current site[s] unless and until approval is given by us.

1.6 In consideration of the undertakings given by you in this letter, we undertake and agree:

    i   to disclose Confidential Information to you;

    ii to keep confidential and not reveal to any person, firm or company (other than persons within the Company who need to know, the Company's bankers and professional advisers) the fact of your investigation into the Company or that discussions or negotiations are taking place or have taken place between yourselves and the Company.

1.7 This letter shall be governed by and construed in accordance with English law and the parties irrevocably submit to the exclusive jurisdiction of the Courts of England and Wales in respect of any claim, dispute or difference arising out of or in connection with this letter.

Please indicate your acceptance of the above by signing and returning the enclosed copy of this letter as soon as possible.

Yours faithfully

ADVISER/VENDOR

We have read and agree to the terms of the above letter.

Signed by: .... Date: ....

For and on behalf of [company sent letter] [Potential Purchaser]

Appendix II: Sample heads of agreement

1.0 The Parties

1.1 The Purchaser is A Buyer Ltd ('the Purchaser').

1.2 The Vendors, at completion, are expected to be as listed in Appendix 1 ('the Vendors').

1.3 The sale assets comprise 100% of the issued share capital of Forsale Limited ('the Company') owned by the Vendors.

2.0 Consideration

2.1 For the entire issued share capital of the Company the consideration will be £6,000,000.

2.2 Consideration will be dependent upon the Company's audited accounts showing a reported Profit Before Interest and Tax of no less than £950,000.

2.3 The Purchaser's parent company, A Buyer plc, where required, will give guarantees as to the funding for the consideration.

2.4 The Consideration will be dependent upon the following conditions:

    i   The Company shall have audited accounts for the year ending 30 April 2002 to enable the Purchaser to confirm before the end of the due diligence process the final items of the 2002 accounts.

    ii Net Assets at completion of £1,400,000. Any variation from this will be dealt with by means of a £1 for £1 adjustment to the total consideration up to a maximum adjustment (up or down) of £200,000. The adjustment will apply to movements upwards and downwards from the above figure.

2.5 Net Assets is defined as the value of the assets of the Company less the value of its liabilities, as shown in the Completion Accounts which will be drawn up from the agreed balance sheet for the period ending at completion. The accounts will be prepared based upon the Company's historical accounting policies.

2.6 The consideration will be satisfied by a combination of:

   i   Cash paid upon completion.
   ii Freely tradable shares in A Buyer plc to a minimum value of £1,000,000 to be issued.
   iii The balance of consideration in Guaranteed Loan Notes, or some other form of instrument at the Vendor's discretion due to their tax planning requirements, issued at completion to the Vendors.

2.7 If Guaranteed Loan Notes are issued as part of the consideration they are to have the following attributes:

   i   They will be issued and redeemed at par.
   ii   All Loan Notes will be allocated to the Vendors proportionate to their individual sale proceeds.
   iii The Loan Notes may be redeemed in multiples of at least £50,000 between the first and fourth anniversary of completion on the giving of 60 days' notice. Any remaining Loan Notes will be automatically redeemed on the fourth anniversary of completion.
   iv   They will attract interest at a rate equivalent to six-month LIBOR, as published by a UK high street bank selected to the satisfaction of the Vendors.
   v   They will be guaranteed by a UK high street bank agreed between the Vendors and the Purchaser.
   vi   They will not be transferable without the Purchaser's consent, except for transfers to family members or family controlled trusts; and
   vii They will contain clauses to ensure they are what are termed 'non-qualifying corporate bonds' for tax purposes.
   viii There will be no rights of set-off against the Loan Notes.

3.0 **Employees**

3.1 Mr Black will resign as Managing Director of the Company on completion, but will make his services available on terms to be agreed, for a reasonable period of time not to exceed one year.

3.2 Notwithstanding 3.1 above, for tax planning purposes it may be required that those Vendors receiving loan notes, or some similar instrument, will be employed by the Company on part-time contracts for the duration of the loan notes.

3.3 The Warrantors will enter into reasonable non-compete agreements with the Purchaser upon completion. The agreements will be restricted to UK jurisdiction and will commence upon completion notwithstanding any employment undertaken by the Directors as required under paragraphs 3.1 and 3.2 above.

4.0 Final Deal Structure

4.1 Both parties will remain flexible with regard to the final deal structure, and respect the other party's taxation and commercial arrangements providing neither party is disadvantaged or is put to any cost. In particular, the Purchaser will allow the transfer of a small amount of shares by the Vendors to their respective family members. This flexibility applies to the structure of the Deal, but not to the Consideration.

5.0 Due Diligence

5.1 The Vendors will provide all reasonable opportunities for the Purchaser and its advisers to conduct such reasonable investigations as are agreed, and subject to the agreement of 'Hold Harmless' letters.

5.2 In the event that the transaction is not completed after the Purchaser and/or its advisors have had access to the names of individual contracts, the Purchaser will not solicit any customers of the Company for a period of 12 months.

6.0 Fees

6.1 Each party will be responsible for their own professional and other costs.

7.0 Confidentiality

7.1 The parties hereby agree that they will keep confidential the matters contemplated by these Heads of Agreement. The Purchaser remains bound by the confidentiality undertaking signed on 24 April 2002 in respect of this proposed transaction.

7.2 None of the parties to this transaction may disclose to any person or company either the fact that discussions or negotiations are taking place between them or any of the contents of these Heads of Agreement or any other terms, conditions or other facts with respect to a possible transaction except as required by law or to their respective advisers, key employees and candidates for senior roles within the post-deal management, provided that they are first informed of the confidential nature of the information. In the case of both key employees and candidates for senior roles within the post-deal management, the Purchaser will first consult with the Vendors.

8.0 Exclusivity

8.1 On signing the Heads of Agreement the Vendors hereby agree not to enter into or continue discussions relating to the sale of the shares with any party other than the Purchaser for a period of 60 days, but if for any reason the transaction is not completed by this date the Vendors reserve the right to enter negotiations with other parties. If at any time the Purchaser advises the Vendor that it does not wish to proceed with the acquisition then the period of exclusivity will end.

9.0 Sale and Purchase Agreement

9.1 The Vendors acknowledge that the Purchaser will require the matters set out in these Heads of Agreement to be incorporated into a legally binding sale and purchase agreement which will contain reasonable warranties and tax indemnities, as are usual for a transaction of the nature and size hereby contemplated and which are mutually agreed between the parties and subject to warranty and indemnity limits noted below and other reasonable limitations.

9.2 The Vendors will remain liable to warranty or indemnity claims brought by the Purchaser up to a maximum aggregate value of the total Consideration. The individual liability of each Vendor will be limited to that Vendor's proportion of Consideration received. The Vendors will give warranties for a period to 31 December 2004. Reasonable aggregate and individual de minimus limits in respect of claims made are to be agreed.

9.3 The Purchaser's solicitors will draft the sale and purchase agreement.

10.0 Subject to

10.1 Contract.

10.2 The Purchaser's satisfaction with due diligence.

11.0 Completion

11.1 Both parties agree that they will progress from the point of signing these Heads of Agreement towards the legal completion, as quickly as is reasonable within the constraints of tax planning and legal requirements. Both parties agree to use reasonable endeavours to complete the transaction within 60 days.

12.0 **Legal Effect**

12.1 In consideration of the further professional costs to be incurred by each party, it is hereby agreed:

i These Heads of Agreement (with the exception of paragraph 5.2, 6, 7 and 8) are not legally binding and shall not create any legal relationship between these parties and are subject to contract and due diligence.

ii Paragraphs 5.2, 6, 7 and 8 are intended to be legally binding between the parties and their construction validity and performance shall be governed by English Law.

Agreed

Shareholder 1   ....

Shareholder 2   ....

Shareholder 3   ....

Shareholder 4   ....

Mr [   ] ....
For and on behalf of A Buyer Ltd

Dated 28 May 2002

APPENDIX 1

Vendors and shareholdings

Name	No. Ordinary £1 Shares
Shareholder 1	13,158
Shareholder 2	1,433
Shareholder 3	1,433
Shareholder 4	2,931
	18,955

Appendix III: Sample due diligence checklist

1. **Organisational structure/history of the company**
   Ownership structure
   Corporate structure (ie subsidiaries, divisions)
   Management structure
   Corporate history
2. **Products/services**
   a. *Types of products*
      Description of product offerings/product lines
      Sales history and market share for each product offering
      Cost/contribution for each product
      Product life cycles
   b. *Raw materials*
      Source of supply and concentration
      Cost (variability, seasonality)
      Major suppliers (number, concentration, dependency)
      Contractual agreements
         specific terms
         cancellation penalty
         current backlog
   c. *Manufacturing process*
      Capacity of plant
      Path of process: raw material to finished product
      Quality control

Sub-contractors
Backlog
d. *Market for products*
Recent growth and outlook
Strategic plans and projection
3. **Marketing**
   a. *Sales force*
   Method of sales (direct vs agents); review of all sales agreements
   Geographic coverage
   Method of sales planning and forecasting
   Location and head count of staff
   Remuneration of sales force
   Distribution channels
   b. *Advertising*
   Media types
   Budgets
   Use of advertising agencies
   c. *Pricing*
   Pricing policies and methods
   Terms of sale
   d. *Customer base*
   List of major customers and their volume (past 3 years)
   Penetration of top customers
   Changes in customer composition
   Customer attrition rate
   Industries served
   Largest customers/degree of credit risk
   Contracts
   Seasonality/cyclicality
   e. *Competitive position: advantages and disadvantages*
   Cost of production/distribution
   Uniqueness of products
   Reputation
   Relationships with customers
   Major competitors
   Competitive factors
   Indirect competition

Potential for future growth in market or market share
Risk of technological obsolescence
4. **Capital expenditures/research and development**
Recent capital expenditures, past 5 years
Planned capital expenditures, next 5 years
Development of new products: history and typical cycle time
R & D budget
5. **Facilities/equipment**
Office or factory locations
Owned vs leased
Lease terms, renewal or purchase options
Estimate of market value of facilities or lease
Maintenance agreements
Expansion capability/capacity utilisation
Proprietary equipment
Depreciation schedules and major equipment listing
6. **Reporting and control systems**
Financial accounting and controls
Stock measurement and control systems
Cost measurement
Production standards
Scheduling
7. **Management**
Personal information on directors and officers, including references
Organisation structure
Employment contracts and remuneration
Incentive plans and fringe benefits
Retirement and pension plans
Reputation and morale
8. **Employees**
Employee count by location and function
Cost of staff, including summary of hourly categories
Details of outsourcing arrangements
Salary packages
Union history: present and past
Union agreements, if applicable
Labour relations
Personnel policies

9. **Litigation**
10. **Patents, trademarks, copyrights and licences**
11. **Governmental regulation**
    Health, safety and environmental issues
    Import issues
12. **Pension and profit sharing plans**
13. **Contingencies**
    Warranties
    Product liability
    Insurance (coverage levels and outstanding claims)
    Disputed taxes
    Contracts/obligations to be assumed
    Off balance sheet liabilities
14. **Financial results**
    a. *Profit and loss account*
       Sales and margin breakdown by product
       Cost of sales
       Overhead and administrative expenses
       Outlook for future, including sensitivity to recession
       Discretionary expenses
    b. *Balance sheet*
       Working capital needs
       Review of debtors (including ageing, concentration and bad debt history)
       Review of stock
       Review of debt/term loans; copies of loan agreements
       Review of prepaid and accrued expenses and accounts
       Review of reserves and customer claims
       Review of fixed assets (type, location, date of acquisition, recent appraisals)
15. **Miscellaneous financial information**
    Forecast profit and loss accounts, including major revenue and cash assumptions
    Auditors' management letters
    Tax status
    Tax and book value of assets
    Depreciation policies (book and tax) for capital assets

Copies of tax computations (3 years)
Previously expensed assets still used

16. **Corporate documents**
    Articles of Incorporation, including all amendments
    Shareholder agreements
    Minutes of all meetings; both directors and shareholders
    Samples of share certificates, share option agreements and any other
    outstanding securities

Appendix IV: Table of contents of a share sale and purchase agreement

1. Recitals

2. Definitions
   Accounts
   Accounts Date
   Act (Companies Act)
   Data Protection Laws
   Bank
   Business Day
   Company
   Completion
   Completion Date
   Completion Net Asset Value
   Computer Systems
   Confidential Information
   Disclosure Letter
   Earn Out Amount
   Escrow
   Financial Reporting Standard
   Income and Corporation Taxes Act

Initial Amount
Intellectual Property
Management Accounts
Proceedings
Property
Purchaser's Solicitors
Restricted Business
Tax Covenants
Vendor's Solicitors
Warranties

3. Agreement for Sale and Purchase
Full title Guarantee
Obligation to Complete

4. Consideration and Completion Accounts
Initial Payment
Earn-out Basis
Net Asset Adjustment
Escrow Account

5. Warranties and Tax Covenants
Capacity
Ownership of Shares
Transfer at Undervalue
Liabilities Owing to or by the Vendors
Memorandum and Articles
Options
Purchase of Own Shares
Statutory Books and Records
Filing of Documents
Insurances
Agency
Compliance with Laws
Licences
Litigation
Insolvency

Fair Trading
Products
Pollution of the Environment
Data Protection
Health and Safety
The Company's Financial Position
Events since Accounts Date
Grants
Debtors
Management Accounts
Borrowings
Continuance of Facilities
Bank Accounts
Guarantees
Assets and Charges
Stocks
Intellectual Property
Plant
Computer Systems
Documents
Material Contract
Defaults
Insider Contracts
Customers/Suppliers
Employee Contracts
Payments on Termination
Redundancies and Transfer of Business
Trade Unions
Incentive Schemes
Pension Schemes
Corporation Tax
Employment Tax
National Insurance
Capital Gains Tax
Stamp Duty
Transfer Pricing
Value Added Tax

6. Warranty Limitations
   Disclosure Letter
   Notice of Claims and Time Limits
   No Prejudice from Prior Investigation
   Right of Contribution
   Maximum and Minimum Amount
   Reduction in Consideration
   Set-off
   Damages

7. Completion
   Delivery of Share Transfer Forms
   Delivery of Statutory Books
   Resignation Notices
   Delivery of Disclosure Letter
   Payment of Monies
   Issuance of Share and Loan Notes

8. Confidential Information and Use of Names

9. Restrictive Undertakings
   Customers
   Employees
   Investment in Competitors

10. Indemnities
    Breach of Covenants

11. General
    Successors
    Whole Agreement
    Waiver
    Law and Jurisdiction
    Counterparts
    Costs
    Severability
    Publicity
    Notices

Schedule 1. The Vendors
2. Details of the Company and Directors
3. Property
4. Pension Scheme
5. Calculation of Completion Net Assets
6. Escrow Account Holders and Terms

Appendix V: Table of contents of an asset purchase agreement

1. Assets to be Purchased and Sold by the Parties
    1.1 Assets to be Purchased by the Buyer
    1.2 Description of Assets
    1.3 Excluded Assets
    1.4 Instruments of Transfer
2. Assumptions of Obligations and Liabilities
    2.1 Assumption of Certain Obligations
    2.2 Details of Liabilities Assumed
3. Purchase Price
    3.1 Consideration
    3.2 Purchase Price to be Paid by the Buyer
        Immediate Cash Payment
        Contingent Cash Payment
    3.3 Allocation
4. Representations and Warranties
    4.1 Buyer's Representations and Warranties
        Authority
        Litigation
        No Conflict or Default
        Complete Disclosure

4.2 Seller's and Shareholders' Representations and Warranties
Authority
Financial Statements
Absence of Certain Changes and Events
Undisclosed Liabilities
Stock
Compliance with Law
Contracts and Commitments
Assets
Title to and Conditions of the Assets
Litigation
No Conflict or Default
Application of Transfer of Undertakings Employment Protection Act
Employee Relations; Employee Remuneration
Key Personnel
Regulatory Approvals
Subsidiaries
Related Party Transactions
Taxes
Accounts Receivable
Environmental Matters
Intellectual Property
Complete Disclosure
5. Covenants
  5.1 Covenant Not to Compete
  5.2 Confidentiality
  5.3 Access
  5.4 Consents and Approval
  5.5 Non-Competition Agreements; Employment Agreements; Consulting Agreements
  5.6 Value Added Tax
  5.7 Bulk Sale
  5.8 Obligations Not Assumed by Buyer
  5.9 Further Assurances
6. Conditions Precedent
  6.1 Conditions Precedent to Obligations of Buyer

Representations and Warranties
Performance of Agreement
No Adverse Change
No Adverse Proceeding
Assignments
Customer Accounts and Lists
Short-Period Audit

6.2 Conditions Precedent to Obligations of Seller and Shareholders
Shareholders
Representations and Warranties
Performance of Agreement
No Adverse Proceeding
Assumption of Obligations

7. Completion
7.1 Completion
7.2 Deliveries by Seller and Shareholders
7.3 Deliveries by Buyer

8. Indemnities
8.1 Survival of Representations, Warranties and Agreements
8.2 Indemnity
8.3 Escrow Agreement; Escrow Deposit
8.4 Procedure for Indemnity with Respect to Third-Party Claims
8.5 Procedure for Indemnity with Respect to Non-Third-Party Claims

9. Miscellaneous Provisions
9.1 Notice
9.2 Entire Agreement
9.3 Binding Effect; Assignment
9.4 Captions
9.5 Fees and Expenses of Transaction
9.6 Waiver; Consent
9.7 No Third-Party Beneficiaries
9.8 Counterparts
9.9 Gender
9.10 Severability
9.11 Remedies Cumulative; Specific Performance
9.12 Governing Law

Schedules and Exhibits Disclosures

Schedule A   Freehold Property
Schedule B   Leasehold Property
Schedule C   Stock
Schedule D   Contracts
Schedule E   Debtors; Deposits and Prepayments
Schedule F   Intellectual Property Rights
Schedule G   Excluded Assets
Schedule H   Excluded Obligations
Schedule I   Allocation of Purchase Price and Assumed Liabilities
Schedule J   Seller's Financial Statements
Schedule K   Certain Change and Events
Schedule L   Litigation
Schedule M   Employee Pension and Profit-Sharing Schemes
Schedule N   Employee Details
Schedule O   Related Party Transactions
Exhibit A   Form of Employment Agreement

Glossary

This section provides definitions of some of the more common words and phrases used in the acquisition process.

Acquisition   The process by which the shares or assets of one company come to be owned by another entity. The transaction may take the form of: 1) a purchase of shares, 2) a purchase of assets and an assumption of liabilities, 3) a reorganisation, 4) a redemption of shares and a recapitalisation, or 5) a merger.

Agent   (see 'Finder' or 'Intermediary') A party authorised to act for either the buyer or the seller in the sale of a business. An agent usually makes an introduction for a fee, but may not carry out negotiations or provide tax advice.

Allocation of Purchase Price   Assignment of the purchase price to individual tangible and intangible assets. Where a premium has been paid over the historic costs of acquired assets, acquirers often either 'step up' the value of tangible assets or apply a part of the purchase price to intangibles, and thus reduce the 'goodwill' element.

Base Cost   The historic cost of an asset. The initial cost plus all additional expenditures and indexation if applicable.

Basket   A minimum threshold of claims which must be reached before any liability is triggered. Buyers seeking post-completion purchase price adjustments typically cannot make claims unless and until their total aggregate damages reach a specified monetary amount, or the 'basket'.

Book Value   The value at which assets and liabilities are recorded on a company's balance sheet.

Break-up Value   The value of a company's assets if sold separately, as in a liquidation.

Buyer/Purchaser/Acquirer   The individual or company who purchases the ownership of the shares in, or assets of, the target.

Capital Gains   Profits from the sale of capital assets. The gain for tax purposes is based on the gross consideration received less the base cost of the ownership.

Capital Structure   A company's net worth plus its interest-bearing debt, as recorded on its balance sheet. The capital structure is the 'foundation' on which a company is built.

Capitalisation Rate   A rate (expressed as a multiple) applied to a company's earnings that reflects both its perceived risks and anticipated earnings growth.

Cash Flow   The excess of all cash sources less all cash uses. Often defined as a company's cash profit plus all non-cash expenses. 'Free cash flow' is defined as cash flow less all capital expenditures (ie, the cash that a company generates after all cash expenditures).

Completion   The consummation of a transaction, when the conditions of a change in ownership are fulfilled and funds are transferred. A completion generally occurs simultaneously with the execution of a sale and purchase agreement, though not always. A sale and purchase agreement may be executed with a completion to follow, pending certain conditions being met.

Consideration   The purchase price for the assets being sold. The consideration is usually cash and/or shares and/or loan notes.

Corporate Finance Adviser   A person or firm that specialises in advising owners of companies on the acquisition or sale or companies. Usually they will find the target and negotiate on behalf of the owner.

Covenant Not to Compete   A covenant found in most sale and purchase agreements, whereby the vendor agrees not to compete with the business being sold for a certain period of time. To enforce non-compete clauses, courts have found that they must be specific in activity, place and time.

Covenants   In a heads of agreement or sale and purchase contract, an agreement to perform or abstain from performing certain actions. Covenants can apply to either party of a transaction, both before and after completion. A typical pre-completion buyer covenant would be to maintain the confidentiality of all negotiations. A typical post-completion vendor covenant would be to agree not to compete in the same business for three years.

Disclosure Requirements   A full listing of disclosures required in any business combination involving a public company. Financial statements in such disclosures must conform to certain principles and standards.

Discounted Cash Flow   An approach to valuation based on discounting a stream of a company's future cash flows to their present value. The rate of discounting is determined by the relative cost of money and the perceived risk (and therefore, premium above the cost of money) inherent in the company.

Due Diligence   An examination by the buyer to confirm that the data provided by the vendor is true, accurate and complete. Due diligence also refers to the review of the vendor's financial statements and examination of the business and legal records. The period of 'due diligence' generally falls after a deal has been negotiated, but before completion.

Earn-out   Additional payments made to vendors contingent on their meeting certain performance goals in the future. Earn-out payments are generally predicated on meeting certain sales or profit levels. Thus, the vendor 'earns out' a portion of the purchase price.

Escrow A 'hold-back' of a portion of the purchase consideration pending fulfilment of certain conditions. Generally, in acquisition matters, buyers demand that a portion of the purchase price be deposited in an escrow account for a certain period pending the outcome of contingent liabilities, such as collection of debtors. Escrow amounts are usually held jointly by the vendor's and buyer's lawyers.

Exclusivity Period A clause in a heads of agreement that restricts the vendor from either soliciting or engaging in discussions with other potential acquirers for a specified time period (usually from 60 to 120 days).

Fair Market Value The value at which an informed buyer will buy and an informed seller will sell, neither under any compulsion to do so.

FIFO The 'First-In, First-Out' inventory cost accounting system. In inflationary times, FIFO inventories are often undervalued.

Finder (See also 'Agent') An individual who introduces a buyer to a seller for a fee. A finder does not work for either side; his role is merely to introduce.

Generally Accepted Accounting Principles ('GAAP') Accepted accounting norms and conditions, as established by the Financial Accounting Standards Board (FASB) in the US and the International Accounting Standards Committee (IASC) in the UK and Western Europe.

Goodwill An intangible asset, representing the excess of the cost of assets over their carried or market value. Goodwill is usually created by purchasing assets at a value higher than their fair market value. Goodwill is essentially 'air'; it represents nothing tangible, only the perceived value of the acquired company's business, reputation and anticipated stream of earnings.

Heads of Agreement ('Letter of intent', 'Memorandum of understanding') A non-binding, written summary of the buyer's and seller's mutual understanding of the price and terms of an acquisition in the process of being negotiated.

Horizontal Integration   The acquisition of other companies in an acquirer's existing field. A 'horizontal merger' is a combination of two companies which produce or sell the same goods.

Illiquid   Not readily convertible into cash.

Indemnification   The assurance by one party that the other party of an agreement will be protected from certain liabilities. In acquisitions, both buyers and sellers generally cross-indemnify each other. Sellers generally indemnify buyers against contingent or undisclosed liabilities; buyers indemnify sellers against claims by lenders or shareholders.

Instalment Sale   A transaction in which at least one payment of a loan note or other obligation is due after the completion .

Intangible Assets   Assets that you cannot physically touch. Intangible assets often appear on company's balance sheet as a result of costs incurred regarding Intellectual Property Rights, patents and the like. Goodwill is also an intangible asset.

Intermediary   ('Investment banker') An adviser who acts for either the buyer or the seller in arranging a transaction. An intermediary is involved in searching for appropriate merger candidates, as well as negotiating and structuring the deal. An intermediary acts as a financial adviser to his client.

Internal Rate of Return ('IRR')   The compound rate of return on an investment in an acquisition, including interest, dividends and capital gains, expressed on a per annum basis. The customary IRR expected by a senior lender is 8–15 per cent; the IRR commanded by equity investors in acquisitions ranges from 20 to 40 per cent.

Leverage   Balancing a relatively large load of debt on a relatively small equity base. To control significant assets through debt. A company with much debt and little equity is considered 'leveraged'.

Leveraged Buy-out ('LBO')   A transaction in which the shares or the assets of a company are purchased primarily through the use of debt. The acquiring entity borrows a substantial part of the acquisition cost against the assets or cash flow of the target company. The acquirer generally uses little or no equity capital in buying the target company, but rather anticipates repayment of debt through either the target's future earnings stream or a separate resale of the target's individual assets.

LIFO   The 'Last-In, First-Out' inventory cost accounting method.

Loan Notes   Notes held by the vendor to help finance an acquisition. Generally, loan notes are unsecured obligations, though they can be secured by a second lien on the assets of the company, or in certain circumstances guaranteed by a bank.

Management Buy-out   A leveraged buy-out (see 'Leveraged Buy-out') in which all or part of a management team buys its company from the shareholders.

Merger   A combination of two businesses into one. In a merger, Company A combines with and disappears into Company B.

Misrepresentation   False or misleading information provided to the other party to a contract.

Non-compete Clause and Non-compete Payment   See 'Covenant Not to Compete'.

Pay-back Period   The time required by a buyer to recoup his original investment in a company through its earnings. Generally, acquirers demand pay-back periods of between five and seven years, taking into account the time value of money.

Pooling of Interests   A method of accounting used in a merger, in which the balance sheets of two companies are combined. No goodwill is recognised on the surviving company's balance sheet, under the premise that no purchase ever occurred. The surviving company's balance sheet also retains the historic cost basis of all assets.

Present Value   The current value of a future payment or stream of payments. Such payments have to be discounted to compensate for the lost current income from, and the uncertainty of, the future payments.

Price/Earnings Ratio ('P/E ratio')   A ratio or multiple derived by dividing the total consideration paid in an acquisition (price) by the acquired company's after-tax earnings (either current or projected). P/E ratios are generated for comparative reasons, to test the relative cost of an acquisition against other like deals.

Principal   A primary investor in an acquisition; one who will hold most of the equity in the acquired company going forward. A principal is distinguished from an adviser, who represents one side in a transaction for a fee.

Purchase Accounting   A method of accounting for an acquisition, in which a purchase price is allocated among the purchased tangible and intangible assets, with the remainder recognised as goodwill.

Recourse   An agreement by a vendor to recompense a buyer for the value of any assets that prove to not be worth their stated value. Recourse arrangements generally apply to the collection of debtors or the obsolescence of inventory.

Representations and Warranties   Binding claims by either party to a transaction. Both buyers and sellers generally warrant certain claims to each other: buyers that they are able to make the acquisition, and sellers as to the nature and condition of their companies.

Sale and Purchase Agreement ('Buy/Sell')   A legally binding contract for the sale of the shares or assets of a company.

Seller/Vendor   The owner of the shares in, or assets of, a company that is subject to disposal.

Senior Debt   Secured debt which has the highest preference to assets in a liquidation.

Stepped-up Basis   The result of increasing the book value of an asset from its historic, depreciated cost to one determined by an acquirer's cost or fair market value.

Subordinated Debt ('Mezzanine Debt')   Debt, often unsecured, which ranks below senior debt but above preferred and common equity in liquidation preference (hence the term 'mezzanine').

Synergy   The creation of greater value by combining two companies than previously existed when they were separate. This can be achieved through a combination of production or marketing skills, or merely a reduction of overhead and an elimination of duplicated systems and staff.

Takeover   Acquiring a controlling interest in a target company, often without the consent of the target company's management.

Target Company   A company that has been selected by a potential acquirer as an attractive candidate.

Term Note   Interest-bearing debt which has a fixed date of maturity.

Vertical Integration   The acquisition of companies engaged in either earlier or later stages of production or marketing. The acquisition of either a supplier or a customer would be a 'vertical' acquisition.

Working Capital   The amount of cash required to fund current assets less current liabilities.

Index

acquirers
  asset purchase where he can allocate purchase price over various assets 91–92
  concept of re-stating your financial statements to reflect 'true' profitability 40, 44
  contingent payments as bonuses or royalties (deductible expenses) 97
  final salary schemes and 52
  financial due diligence prior to buying a company 45–46
  operating costs and 48
  part of purchase price allocated to a non-compete 96
  pay 'premium' for growth of earnings 39
  relevant data they need 73
  same people who developed company will remain to run it 50
  share purchase maintains balance sheet intact 91
  up-to-date acturial report from independent actuary 52, *see also* buyers
acquisitions, cash payments made by bank transfer 119
actuary, current value of final salary pension scheme and 52
Alternative Investment Market of the London Stock Exchange (AIM) 23–24
American Stock Exchange 25
amortisation options, loan notes and 95
asset approach, appropriate for companies with tangible assets 34
auction process, marketing your company 78–79
average price/earnings ratio for acquisition targets, doubled between (1979–1989) 19

'balloon' payments 95
banks, reluctant to lend enough capital for aggressive growth rates 17
'basket', definition 116–17
before considering a sale
  address environmental problems 51–52
  advantageous to fix problems 21
  build management team for transition 50
  codify and strengthen legal and contractual affairs 48–49
  confront pension issues 52
  establish adequate systems and controls 50–51
  polish your physical plant 46–48
  position your financial statements to your advantage 44
    clean up your stock and debtors 46
    get audited statements 45–46
    straighten out your financial affairs 44–45
  straighten out your records 49–50
Blanc, Francois 131, 134–37
'book value', definition 34
brokers, work for the 'deal' 56
business value, difference between values of underlying assets is goodwill 35
buyers
  can ascertain when business's fortunes are about to go downward 21
  cautious about income capitalisation 38
  circumstances and objectives may be at odds with sellers 91
  concern you are selling because of some imminent problem with business 82
  conservative about future prospects of company 96

convinced of significant growth possibility to pay high multiple 36
determine valuations 31
draft heads of agreement to spell out the 'intent' 103
draft sale and purchase agreement 110
due diligence and 109, 116
environmental audits and 51
exclusivity clause 104
form of non-compete 96, 114
indemnity section in sale and purchase document 115
initially refuse to consider a basket 117
look at company from perspective of 53
potential will eventually unearth all the facts 75
presentation materials and 73
protection from contingent, undisclosed liabilities 112
require indemnity from tax problems arising from your actions 44
'shy away' from deal with too few assets and too much goodwill 35, 92
sincere interest in selling and 69
want to be confident that company can survive its owner 50
ways to make meetings with successful 81
will not pay for efficiencies or synergies 40
willing to pay premiums for companies that have systems and controls 50
buyers' psychology, subject to perceptions of state of the world 18

Canam
Blanc of visited Advanced Technologies 131
chairman of spent day with Tom Ward but still no offer (6 May 2002) 132
Lam (Advanced solicitor) protested about warranty clause 135
new financial adviser appointed by Chris Smith 136
offered £30 million in cash for Advanced 133, 134
purchase agreement writing started despite Lam 135
sale agreed (27 September 2002) 136–37
capital equipment, cyclical industry 20
capital gain on sale of shares, apportioned between business asset gains and non-business asset gains 100
Capital Gains Tax 24, 99–101

capitalisation rate, annualised return an investor should expect from investment 36
case study of Advanced Technologies Ltd 121
balance sheet 123
brief history 121–23
confidentiality agreements with firms 128
mandate to sell on exclusive basis for nine months 128
'market researchers' tour company 125
meeting with the Board 126
operating results 122
problem over warranty about undisclosed liabilities 135
sale and purchase agreement resolved 27 September 2002 136
sent out more memorandum 129
short video of the plant 129
slipping performance 135–36
special Board meeting (17 May 2002) 133
summary of offers for 134
cash deal, cleanest method of payment 94
chambers of commerce 64
Charles Holdings, interested in Advanced but had money problem 132, 134
Clark, William, visit to Advanced Technologies 130, 133
clients
Birmingham-based distributor of industrial products, valuation and price 32
clothing company with trademarked names and failure of deal 118
company with difficult of succession owned by two brothers and an uncle 13–15
company that manufactured lighting fixtures, deal 'shop soiled' 70
company with tradition of employment contracts every April Fool's Day 48
copper in soil from munitions factory 51
distributor of electronic parts and stock control system 48
distributor of hydraulic components, sold to well-funded private equity group 37–38
finding about one with reported negligible profits 39–40
manufacturer of medical diagnostic equipment, focus on product liability 89
manufacturer of processing equipment for petroleum industry 18
medical products company with difficulty of succession 15
one who insisted no buyer more important than running of his business 81–82

plastic-moulding business with car-wash and 45
precision aluminium casting company, advantage of sale of 16
sale of company producing drill bits for oil industry (1980s) 20–21
tyre distribution business client, administrative costs 18
Collins Stevant stockbrokers, analysts of 26
company
  address miscellaneous financial aspects 45
  'cash' business and discretionary cash 44
  little 'free float' in its shares and liquidity 26
  opportunity to clinch deal is fleeting 22
  those outside your field are willing to 'pay up' 76
  value goals prior to marketing your 42
comparative companies, choose universe of similar 36–37
comparisons, easier said than done 36
competitors, bidding for your business 76–77
completion, the 117–19
confidentiality 60, 72, 78, 80, 128, 139–46
contingent earn-outs, when owner staying to run company after sale 97
control over operations and strategic planning 25, 27–28
controlled sale of company 79
Corporation Tax, P/E ratio and 35
covenants, maintaining the status quo at the selling company 113
Cranfield School of Management 13
'critical mass' 25, 37
cross-border transactions, drop in 2001 and 2002 28

deal, the 90
  structure 71, 90–93
  tax considerations 99
    capital gains tax 99–102
    inheritance tax 102
  terms 94–95
    contingent payments/earn-outs 96–98
    employment and consultancy agreements 95–96
    loan notes 95
    payments for covenants not to compete 96
    pension payments 96
    shares 98–99
debt-to-equity ratios 35
depreciation 98
discount rate, definition 38

due diligence 45–46, 98, 108–10, 116, 136

earn-outs 96–98, 117
employees, only inform those who need to know of sale 82
employment payments, deductible providing buyers with tax benefits 95
escrow accounts 89–90, 117
'exclusive agreement', definition 66
'exclusive' window of time 104

fair market value 31, 34
'family businesses', hope of family dynasty 13
financial analysts, penalize companies that have too much goodwill on balance sheets 92
financial markets, global in nature 76
firms, pay 'premiums' to gain foothold in a field 38
flotation
  control and 25, 27–28
  generates capital to fund company's growth plans 25, 27
  private company becomes a public one 24
  stability of the markets and 25, 28–29
flotation on a stock market (initial public offering) (IPO) 23

general business and financial markets, IPO and M&A markets tied to 28
'goodwill' 35, 92
Grant Thornton 13
growth possibilities of your company 25, 27
guaranteed loan note 95

Haagen-Dazs 27
heads of agreement ('letter of intent') 103–06, 107
  due diligence procedures and 109
  issues
    conditions and contingencies of the deal 105
    price and terms of the deal 104
    specifics of any employment agreements, consulting agreements or covenants not-to-compete 105
    structure of the deal 105
    time frame for negotiating the purchase agreement 105
    legal adviser and 105
Hewlett-Packard, comparison with £25 million manufacturer of tests instruments 37
house price example 37
housing, cyclical industry 20

income capitalisation model, difficulty in
  preparing   38
indemnities   44, 115–17
indemnity, duration of   116
indexation of shares   99
industry associations   64
information memorandum, sample   75
Inheritance Tax   24, 102
initial 'down payment', satisfaction with   98
Inland Revenue, clearance of the transaction
  by   115
Inspector of Taxes, tax deed and warranties
  indemnified for 7 years   116
Institute of Directors   64
'interest only' periods   95
International Stamping, interest in Advanced
  Technologies   129, 134
'inventory cushions'   44
'invest in taxes' for a year or two   45
IPO market, significantly more volatile   28
Iraq War, international trade and   20

James, Anne, Advanced Technologies and   126,
  134

Kellogg, Beth (middle daughter in Smith family)
  126–27
Klein, Janet (Chris Smith's eldest sister), Director's
  fee and   124–25, 127

Lam, Bill (solicitor for Advanced Technologies)
  135–36
letter of engagement, adviser and   66
letter of intent, issues covered by   104–05
Lindsay Industries, Advanced Technologies
  and   131, 134
loan note is non-QCB, qualify for taper relief   101
loan notes   95, 101, 117
'lock-in' arrangement, liquidity and   26, 98

macro or general economic environment   18, 20
Main Market, appropriate for larger companies
  (market capitalisation of more than (£100
  million))   23
management buyout   72
managing directors   24, 26, 28
market comparison approach, selling your
  business   35, 37
markets   72, 79–80
  reward larger companies with higher multiples
    because of 'critical mass'   37
Marx, Karl   41

merger and acquisition activity, high correlation
  between general economic growth and   19
merger market   29, 33, 35
merger specialists, elaborate models to refine key
  variables   38

NASDAQ   25
negotiating environment, always maintain a
  positive   89
negotiations
  compromise and   86
  never over till deal closes   108
  third party to negotiate initial stages   89
new flotation or Initial Public offering   28
New York Stock Exchange   25
non-compete covenants   96, 114
'non-exclusive agreement', definition of   66
non-qualifying assets, removed from the company
  in advance of sale   107
non-recurring expenses   98

Official List of the London Stock Exchange   23
on-going capital expenditures   98
'opportunistic' buyers, those who will buy at
  distressed prices   70
optimal deal
  structuring and negotiating   85–90
    be flexible   87
    deal honestly and openly   88
    do not expect to win every battle   86
    do not get emotional   87
    do not over-negotiate   88
    keep your eyes on your goals   86
    listen   88
    never be afraid to walk away from a deal
      88
    never threaten to walk away from a deal
      unless you mean it   88
    understand the other side's wants and
      needs   87
Orvis, Herbert (Charles Holdings)   131, 133
outlook of your company's industry   18, 20
owners
  believe their companies should be valued on
    intangible benefits   34
  faith in their negotiating skills   85
  important to move quickly when IPO markets
    are hot   28–29
  often stay on to run the company after sale   16
  preparatory actions for selling   43
  some provide excruciating detail which is
    mistake   74

stance that 'anything is for sale at right
      price'   70
take eyes off the running of company in
      anticipation of sale   84
tax-avoidance schemes and   44–45
too close to their businesses to be rational in
      assessing situations   89
unrealistic high values on their businesses   42
what they want   72

P/E multiples, gauge investor sentiment towards
      economy and your company   36
Peel Hunt stockbrokers, analysts to follow and
      research shares   26
'peer' group, comparison of operating ratios   36
People and Relationship Issues in Management
      (PRIMA service)   13
potential acquirers   33
price, two parties, a buyer and seller agree   31
price/book value ratios   35
price/earnings ratios (P/E)   35
price/sales ratios   35
private companies
      breaches of warranties and   116
      cost of obtaining a listing   24
      flotation not viable   24–25
      little or no public data exists   37
      markets for rise and fall   18
      merger activity doubled from 1979to 1989   19
      risky illiquid investments   36
      small amounts of capital and   15
      supress reported profits for tax purposes   39
private company's 'return', reinvested back in
      illiquid investment   15
product liability claims, large three-year escrow
      and   89–90
professional corporate finance advisers
      acquisition criteria of active buyers and   77
      advantages of   102–03
      confidentiality and   60
      definition and role   55–56
      experience and objectivity of   56
      experience of   62
      focused effort of   62–63
      knowledge of buyers   60
      personal compatibility of   64
      professional information memorandum on your
            company   73–74
      professionalism of   62
      representing only sellers   63–64
      role as a buffer   61–62
      selecting an adviser   64–65

senior level attention of   63
      sensitivity to your objectives   63
      skill at negotiations   60–61
      terms and fees for   65–67
'professional' managers   14
profit and loss account, necessary to go through on
      line-by-line basis   39
profit-avoiding schemes, arm's length financial
      audit and   46
property leases and contracts binding the company
      49
prospects in the market   22
psychologists, first impressions and ultimate
      perception of situation   80–81

qualifying corporate bonds (QCB)   101

reasons for selling   5
      association with a larger company   5, 17–18
      diversification of assets   5, 15–16
      expansion capital and   5, 17
      retirement or reduction of time spent in the
            business   6, 12
      succession concerns   5, 12–15
      timing   5, 18–22
relative prospects and performance of your
      company   18, 21
return on assets (profits/assets)   35
return on equity (profits/shareholders' equity)
      35
return on sales (profits/sales)   35
risk, major plant expansion or new product
      development and   15–16
sale
      can provide continued access to capital through
            its parent   27
      eliminates all on-going business risk   25
      leaves you with only minor participation in
            future growth   26
      liquidity and   25–26
      versus flotation   23–25
      you will lose total command over your
            company   27
sale process   69–71
      create a market   78
            use confidentiality agreements   80
            use third party to make initial approaches
                  79–80
      establish goals and strategies   71–73
      identify prospective buyers   76–77
      keep the business going   82, 84

liquidity and diversification from 16
outside your industry 76–77
prepare presentation materials 73–76
reasons for selling 5
requires effort 70–71
sample of contents for information memorandum 75
sell, sell, sell 80–82
typical sale should take from six to nine months 72–73
typical timetable/chronology of 83
sale and purchase agreement 107–08, 110
conditions for completion 114–15
covenants 113–14
indemnities 115–17
price, terms and structure of the deal 111
representations and warranties 111–13, *see also* Appendix IV
sales of private (middle-market companies), not all-cash deals 94
SARS epidemic, international trade and 20
sellers
advantages for to enter into heads of agreement 104
attempt to sell their companies 'as is' 112
indemnities 116
negotiations and emotional wear and tear on 89
only liable for claims based on significant problems 116
optimistic about future prospects 96
optimistic about income capitalisation 38
prefer a share transaction to asset transaction 93
warranty issues 112–13
September 11 (2001), international trade and 20
share purchase 91, 92–93
'sharing of power', difficult to effect 14
small companies, growing capital demands and 17
Smith, Caroline (wife of Chris Smith) 127
Smith, Chris (son of James and MD of Advanced Technologies) 122, 124–25, 127, 131, 135–37
Smith, James (founder of Advanced Technologies) 121–22, 127
Spencer, Robert (owner of Spensports) 6, 12, 17, 20
Spensports 6, 17, 20
start-ups, worth relatively little 16
Stock exchange, public companies required to publish interim reports 24
Stock Exchange-listed retailer, Spensport and 6

Stock market and AIM, 2, 400 public listed 25
stock market FTSE 100 peaked at 6930 (December 1999) 20
strategic trade-offs. successful negotiated deals and 86
strategy to achieve goals 72
sudden death, succession concerns and 12–13

taper relief 99–101
tax 24, 35, 44, 49, 99–102
tax-avoidance schemes 44
'terms and conditions', advisable to codify and formalise 49
trade and asset purchase 91–92
asset deal more complex and expensive 93
cost 93
liabilities and 93
taxes and 93
trade-offs to attain your primary goals 85–86
transactions, done in the concrete 31
transfer of assets between husband and wife, no gain/no loss rule 107
true value of company, determined by the market 31
trust, to change ownership of shares 107
'tyre kickers' or sellers who are not really serious 69

UK Treasury Notes, 'riskless' investments 36
under-funded pension scheme, hurdle between seller and deal 52
United Kingdom
number of flotations varies widely each year 28
two main stock markets 23
unsecured loan note 95
US Securities Act (1933), 'full and fair disclosure' 108

valuations
can give idea of what range of prices you might expect 31–32
done in the abstract 31
methods 33–34
discounted cash flow (DCF) 33, 38–39
multiple of income basis 33, 35–38
underlying asset value 33, 34–35
profit 39–40
value
always determined in the margin 37
defined in terms of cash or cash equivalents 32–33

determined by combination of numerous elements   33, 39
interplay between company's assets and its profits   35
key to is ability to generate earnings   39
myths about   40
  'Just gimme my price' theory   41–42
  labour theory of   41
  revenue theory of   41
what company is worth   31–33

Ward, Tom
  against selling to Charles but left decision to family   132
  became MD of Advanced Technologies (2000)   122

called for professional advice (15 January 2002)   124
chose Canam   134
day with Herbert Orvis   131
met David Wilding (12 March 2002)   129
presided over Board meeting   123
provision of historical statements by   125
rumour he had been offered MD job elsewhere   127
sent information requested and memorandum drawn up   128
six months after completion upbeat about business   137
ways to acquire a business   91
Wilding, David, dealings with Advanced Technologies   129–33
world economies stagnant (1970s)   19

Printed in the United States
105199LV00002B/214/A

9 780749 444570